100% de réussite en anglais

Claude Gosset

3e

EDITIONS OPHRYS

COMMENT UTILISER 100% DE RÉUSSITE

Ce cahier va t'aider à mieux comprendre ce que tu apprends en classe, à mieux participer en cours, à préparer efficacement tes contrôles, en un mot à devenir meilleur en anglais.

SOIS RÉGULIER, C'EST LE SECRET !

100% de réussite se compose de **12 unités** et de **6 bilans** qui reprennent **l'essentiel du programme**. Le plus facile pour toi est de faire les chapitres dans l'ordre, car nous avons suivi la progression habituelle des manuels.

CALCULE TON SCORE DE RÉUSSITE POUR CHAQUE UNITÉ

En multipliant par deux le total obtenu dans les tests, tu obtiendras un pourcentage qui reflétera ton niveau. **Toutes les réponses sont dans le livret des corrigés.**

UN POINT DE GRAMMAIRE TE POSE PROBLÈME ?

Regarde au dos de ton cahier ! Reporte-toi à la fiche **REMEMBER !** correspondante, fais les tests et vérifie avec les corrigés.

6 BILANS POUR PRÉPARER LES CONTRÔLES

Fais **en une seule fois** chacun des tests **JE FAIS LE POINT...** Ils correspondent aux contrôles de mi-trimestre ou de fin de trimestre (*octobre, décembre, février, mars, mai, juin*) que l'on donne en classe. Tu verras tes notes grimper !

12 UNITÉS POUR PROGRESSER

À L'ORAL

Repère les tests précédés de PISTE 2 dans la partie **JE COMPRENDS CE QUE J'ENTENDS**. Écoute ton CD et coche les cases « vrai/faux » ou complète les mots manquants. Les dialogues ou phrases enregistrés ne dépassent pas 2 minutes ! Et pour te rassurer..., tous les textes des dialogues sont aussi dans le **livret des corrigés**.

ET À L'ÉCRIT

Entraîne-toi avec **JE COMPRENDS CE QUE JE LIS** et teste ton niveau de compréhension. Et **pour t'assurer que tu sais t'exprimer** réponds aux questions, complète les textes ou traduis les phrases de **JE COMPRENDS ET J'ÉCRIS**.

ET POUR APPRENDRE TOUT EN S'AMUSANT

GAMES ! DES JEUX !

Tu trouveras aussi des mots-croisés, des phrases mystères, des mots à associer.

BON COURAGE ET BEAUCOUP DE SUCCÈS !

SOMMAIRE

ISBN : 978-2-7080-1212-7

Éditions Ophrys
25, rue Ginoux - 75015 Paris
www.ophrys.fr

Édition coordonnée par **Sylvie Persec**
conception graphique et réalisation **céline farez _ virginie rio**
illustrations **Catherine Beaumont**

▸ LE PRÉSENT SIMPLE
▸ *BE*
▸ *HAVE*

unit 1

Do you like sushi?

JE COMPRENDS CE QUE J'ENTENDS

PISTE 2

1 True or false?

Écoute cette conversation et dis si ces phrases sont vraies ou fausses.

	True	False
1. Patty and Andy are neighbours.		
2. They both live in Liverpool.		
3. Andy feels quite at home here.		
4. Vancouver is an American town.		
5. Patty's father makes video games.		
6. Andy's mother works in a restaurant.		
7. Andy's mother is of Japanese origin.		
8. Her restaurant is in London Street.		
9. Andy works with his father on Saturdays.		
10. Patty's looking for a job.		

MON SCORE | 10

REMEMBER!

LE PRÉSENT SIMPLE

Ce temps permet de **parler de ce qui est vrai à tout moment**. Il sert à **donner des définitions** d'ordre général. *The Earth revolves around the Sun.* La terre tourne autour du soleil.
Il permet de **caractériser une personne par ses goûts ou ses habitudes.** *He likes football.* Il aime le football. *She often goes shopping on Saturdays.* Elle fait souvent du shopping le samedi.
Il sert à **exprimer des opinions.** *I don't think you're right.* Je ne pense pas que tu aies raison. *Do you agree with her?* Es-tu d'accord avec elle ?
Il permet aussi de **parler de ce qui est prévu** dans un emploi du temps. *Our plane takes off at 8:30.* Notre avion décolle à 8h30.

PISTE 3

2 Listen and write.

Écoute et copie ces 5 phrases en t'aidant des mots fournis.

1. School ....
2. How often ....?
3. I ....
4. .... *the net.*
5. Great Britain ....

MON SCORE | 5

REMEMBER!

BE (voir liste des verbes irréguliers sur le rabat de droite)

• **Le verbe *BE*** s'emploie pour **parler de soi** *My name's Andy.* Je m'appelle Andy. *I'm from Canada.* Je suis originaire du Canada. *I'm 16.* J'ai 16 ans.
et pour **parler de ce que l'on ressent** *I'm hungry, thirsty, cold, warm.* J'ai faim, soif, froid, chaud.
• **L'auxiliaire *BE*** est utilisé **avec la forme en *–ing* du verbe**, au présent et au passé,
It's raining. Il pleut *It was raining.* Il pleuvait.
et pour **former la voix passive** *Most toys are made in China.* La plupart des jouets sont fabriqués en

3 Translate these sentences.

MON SCORE | 5

Traduis ces phrases.

1. *She was angry with me.* ....
2. *Were they still dancing at midnight?* ....
3. *Is the text translated into French?* ....
4. *She's 17, isn't she?* ....
5. *It's cold today.* ....

4 Are you good at science?

Trouve la définition correspondant à chacun de ces cinq termes.

carbon dioxide / environment / greenhouse effect / ozone layer / photosynthesis

1. *The conditions and area where something exists or lives.* → ....
2. *The process in which carbon dioxide and other gases warm the surface of the earth...*
→ ....
3. *A gas that heats up our atmosphere and absorbs oxygen.* → ....
4. *The process that plants use to turn carbon dioxide into oxygen.* → ....
5. *A layer of the Earth's atmosphere that shields Earth from the Sun's ultraviolet rays.*
→ ....

MON SCORE | 5

5 5. a, b or c?

Que sais-tu du monde anglophone ?

1. *The United Kingdom consists of England, Wales, Scotland and a. the Highlands. / b. Iceland. / c. Northern Ireland.*
2. *Two of the United States of America have no common border with the other 48 states. They are Alaska and a. the Hawaian Islands. / b. the Bahamas. / c. the Orkney Islands.*
3. *Admiral Nelson won the battle of Trafalgar on 21st October 1805 but that day he a. lost an eye. / b. got killed. / c. lost an arm.*
4. *They don't use dollars in a. Canada. / b. Great Britain. / c. New Zealand.*
5. *The Americans elect a new president every a. year. / b. six years. / c. four years.*
6. *The English cut their king's head off in 1649. His name was a. James I. / b. Charles I. / c. Henry I.*

7. The American banknotes are a. blue. / b. yellow. / c. green.

8. If you want to write to the Prime Minister in London you must send your letter to a. Buckingham Palace. / b. 221b Baker Street. / c. 10 Downing Street.

9. One of these American presidents was not assassinated: a. Abraham Lincoln. / b. Frank Delano Roosevelt. / c. William McKinley.

10. Natives Indians sold Manhattan to the Americans in 1626 for a. $24. / b. $30,000,000. / c. $100,000.

MON SCORE | /10

JE SAIS M'EXPRIMER

REMEMBER!

HAVE

Le verbe *HAVE* et la tournure *HAVE GOT* permettent de parler de **ce que l'on possède.**
I have a motorbike. / I've got a motorbike. J'ai une moto.
Les formes négatives et interrogatives sont différentes. *I don't have any sisters. / I haven't got any sisters.* Je n'ai pas de sœurs. *Do you have any sisters? / Have you got any sisters?* As-tu des sœurs ?
HAVE s'emploie comme un verbe ordinaire dans les expressions suivantes :
Have breakfast, lunch, tea, dinner. Prendre son petit déjeuner, déjeuner, prendre le thé, dîner.
Have a lesson, a shower, a bath. Prendre un cours, une douche, un bain.
What time do you have dinner? À quelle heure dines-tu ?
L'auxiliaire *HAVE* s'emploie avec le participe passé des verbes pour **former le *present perfect*** (unité 6) **et le *past perfect*** (unité 7).
Rappel : le participe passé d'un verbe régulier se forme en ajoutant *-ed* à sa base verbale :
work → ***worked*** / *decide* → ***decided*** *I have finished my work.* J'ai terminé mon travail.
Le participe passé d'un verbe irrégulier est le 3ᵉ terme de la liste sur le rabat de droite.
write → *wrote* → ***written*** *Have you drunk your tea?* As-tu bu ton thé ? *They had gone when I arrived.* Ils étaient partis quand je suis arrivé.

6 Translate these sentences.

MON SCORE | /5

Traduis ces phrases.

1. J'ai un cours de maths tous les jours. ....
2. Il ne vient pas très souvent. ....
3. Combien de frères as-tu ? ....
4. Combien y-a-t-il de secondes dans une semaine ? ....
5. Où déjeunes-tu le lundi ? ....

7 Complete these sentences.

MON SCORE | /5

Complète ces phrases à l'aide de *BE* ou *HAVE* au temps qui convient.

1. He wants to know if my sister .... all right.
2. I .... thirsty. Give me something to drink.
3. – Does he .... children ? – Yes, he does.
4. They .... finished working when the film began.
5. I don't know where he can .... at the moment.

8 What's the opposite.

Dis le contraire.

MON SCORE | 5

1. I'm interested in giraffes.

....

2. There aren't any tigers in China.

....

3. My sister wasn't at home last night at 11.

....

4. She works in a bank.

....

5. My doctor doesn't smoke.

....

CALCULE TON TAUX DE RÉUSSITE SUR CE CHAPITRE

Entre 100% et 80%, tu as tout compris. BRAVO !
Entre 80% et 60%, c'est bien.
Si tu as moins de 60%, refais les tests dans quelques jours.

1: | 10
\+ 2: | 5
\+ 3: | 5
\+ 4: | 5
\+ 5: | 10
\+ 6: | 5
\+ 7: | 5
\+ 8: | 5

| 50

x 2 =

% de réussite

DES JEUX ! GAMES!

Trouve dans cette grille 24 phrases de première nécessité en rayant les lettres inutiles comme dans la première ligne. Les mots ne sont pas séparés. Les phrases sont toutes écrites horizontalement. Il y en a une par ligne.

~~A~~	~~R~~	~~T~~	~~F~~	~~T~~	~~E~~	T	H	A	N	K	S	A	L	O	T	~~R~~	~~G~~							
W	E	L	C	O	M	E	T	O	E	N	G	L	A	N	D	N	S							
H	R	T	Y	Y	H	A	V	E	A	N	I	C	E	D	A	Y	X							
W	H	E	R	E	A	R	E	Y	O	U	F	R	O	M	G	G	H							
T	H	E	J	E	W	O	I	M	S	O	R	R	Y	M	A	L	T							
P	L	E	A	S	E	D	T	O	M	E	E	T	Y	O	U	I	A							
A	U	C	L	A	H	O	W	O	L	D	A	R	E	Y	O	U	I							
N	E	N	J	O	Y	Y	O	U	R	S	E	L	F	A	M	I	P							
C	A	N	Y	O	U	R	E	P	E	A	T	P	L	E	A	S	E	H	A	T	I	S	C	V
L	E	N	D	M	E	Y	O	C	A	N	I	H	E	L	P	Y	O	U	P	E	N	S	O	T
A	Q	W	S	P	E	L	L	Y	O	U	R	N	A	M	E	Z	S	X	E	F	V	R	F	B
T	P	I	R	E	R	Y	O	U	C	A	N	T	S	M	O	K	E	H	E	R	E	B	G	C
G	F	W	H	A	T	S	Y	O	U	R	P	H	O	N	E	N	U	M	B	E	R	T	H	J
H	V	H	J	Y	C	A	N	I	S	E	E	Y	O	U	R	P	A	S	S	P	O	R	T	J
B	N	O	P	A	R	K	I	N	G	B	N	J	K	I	U	Y	T	R	A	S	X	C	V	B
G	F	H	U	I	R	T	W	H	A	T	A	B	O	U	T	A	D	R	I	N	K	S	P	H
A	R	E	Y	O	U	O	K	N	A	P	O	L	E	O	W	E	L	L	I	G	T	O	O	N
C	A	E	R	T	T	E	A	O	R	C	O	F	F	E	E	N	E	L	D	S	O	G	B	N
G	O	O	D	M	O	R	N	I	N	G	A	Z	E	R	T	Y	U	I	I	O	P	M	K	G
Q	S	D	F	W	H	A	T	S	Y	O	U	R	J	O	B	S	D	G	H	J	K	T	I	M
W	I	L	D	I	A	S	H	A	S	E	E	Y	O	U	L	A	T	E	R	K	E	S	P	O
C	H	A	R	I	D	O	N	T	U	N	D	E	R	S	T	A	N	D	D	I	C	J	K	E
S	U	P	E	R	T	H	I	N	A	P	M	R	C	V	H	O	W	D	O	Y	O	U	D	O
T	E	R	V	I	C	T	O	R	D	O	N	O	T	D	I	S	T	U	R	B	N	E	M	O

Unit 2

- **LE PRÉSENT EN *BE+ING***
- ***CAN, MUST, MAY***
- ***YES/NO AND OR-QUESTIONS***

Why aren't you working?

JE COMPRENDS CE QUE J'ENTENDS

PISTE 4

1 True or false?

MON SCORE ____ | 10

Écoute ce dialogue et trouve la bonne réponse.

	True	False
1. Mike is pleased to get a phone call.		
2. Mike is cooking.		
3. Anne is surprised because Mike is cooking.		
4. Mike is making eleven pizzas.		
5. Mike plays rugby.		
6. Mike and his team are celebrating their victory.		
7. Mike could buy ready-made pizzas. Nobody would mind.		
8. Anne would like to be invited.		
9. A pizzaiolo is a cook specialised in pizzas.		
10. You're invited to Mike's party.		

REMEMBER!

LE PRÉSENT EN *BE+ING*

Le présent en *be+ing* se forme avec *be* suivi de la forme en *-ing* du verbe : *He's sleeping.* Il dort. (Il est en train de dormir.)

Il s'emploie **pour parler d'une action qui a lieu au moment où l'on parle.** *Your dog's eating my cat!* Ton chien est en train de manger mon chat !

pour décrire un document. *On this photo she is wearing a leather jacket.* Sur cette photo elle porte une veste en cuir.

pour décrire la position d'un personnage *He's lying on the ground.* Il est allongé sur le sol.

pour parler d'un événement futur prévu, généralement associé à un mot renvoyant au futur. *We're going to Australia next summer.* Nous allons en Australie l'été prochain.

pour porter un jugement (souvent négatif) *He's sleeping again!* Il est encore en train de dormir ! *You're always fighting!* Vous êtes tout le temps en train de vous battre !

PISTE 5

2 Listen and write.

Écoute et complète ces phrases.

1. Queen Elisabeth .... *to Balmoral* ....

2. Your panther' .... *on my coat!*

3. The All Blacks .... *for Europe* ....

4. They .... *to my party* ....

5. What .... *you* .... *about?*

MON SCORE ____ | 5

REMEMBER!

CAN, MUST, MAY

Can, must et *may* sont des auxiliaires. Ils sont suivis d'une base verbale (verbe sans *to*). ***MUST*** exprime **une obligation, un ordre** et, à la forme négative, ***MUSTN'T***, **une interdiction**. *You must go home.* Il faut que tu rentres chez toi. *You mustn't turn right!* Tu ne dois pas tourner à droite (il est interdit de...)
CAN/CAN'T sert à exprimer **la possibilité / l'impossibilité**, ou la **permission / l'interdiction**.
I can't sleep. Je ne peux pas dormir. (je n'arrive pas à dormir)
You can't smoke in a hospital. Tu ne peux pas fumer dans un hôpital.
MAY exprime **une autorisation ou une demande de permission**.
Mum, may I go out tonight? Puis-je sortir ce soir ?
MAY, MUST* et *CAN/CAN'T permettent aussi de dire qu'un événement est **plus ou moins possible ou probable**. *It may be your friend Anna.* Il se peut que ce soit ton amie Anna. *It must be Peter.* Ce doit être Peter. *It can't be Peter.* Il est impossible que ce soit Peter.

3 True or false?

Ces affirmations sont-elles vraies ou fausses ?

Sue: *Sam. Wake up!*
Sam: *What's the matter, Sue?*
Sue*: Can't you hear? Someone is snoring.*
I can't sleep! You must do something. It must be Peter.
Sam*: But what can I do?*
Sue*: He's your brother. Go and tell him.*
Sam*: It can't be Peter. I'm sure my brother doesn't snore.*
But, let me think, it may be your friend, Anna, after all!
She's in the tent on the right. Now, leave me alone and go back to sleep.
Sue*: But, Sam I...*
Anna: *Hey! Can't you two stop talking? I can't sleep!*
Sue*: Shut up, Anna! You're snoring!*

	True	*False*
1. Sam and Sue are camping.		
2. Sam is asleep.		
3. Sue can't sleep because Sam is snoring.		
4. Peter is Sam's cousin.		
5. Sue wants Sam to go and tell Peter to stop snoring.		
6. Anna is Sue's friend.		
7. Anna is sleeping in a tent next to Sam and Sue's.		
8. Sue goes out and can hear Anna snoring.		
9. Anna wakes up because Sam and Sue are talking.		
10. In the end Sue is angry with her cousin Anna.		

4 Translate these sentences.

Traduis ces phrases.

1. Cats can't swim and dogs can't climb up trees. ....
2. No one answers the phone. They must be out. ....

3. Can I have some coffee, please? .... ?

4. I'm fed up! I can't do anything in this house! ....

5. Look at that man over there! Do you think he can be one of the Xmen actors?

.... ?

6. No, you mustn't use your father's car. You haven't got enough experience. ....

....

7. I can't take you to the disco tonight. I don't have any money. ....

....

8. Harry and Hermione! You must learn how to use your magic wands properly.

.... !

9. A red kangaroo can jump up to 10 feet. ....

10. He phoned ten minutes ago. He may be late. ....

MON SCORE | 10

JE SAIS M'EXPRIMER

5 Answer these questions.

Fais des réponses courtes.

1. – Is your brother watching the Simpsons?

– Yes, ...

2. – Are there French fries for dinner?

– No, ...

3. – Can I help you?

– Yes, ...

4. – Do you speak Spanish, Juanita?

– Of course.. !

5. – May I use your car, Mum?

– Yes, ...

MON SCORE | 5

REMEMBER!

YES-NO QUESTIONS

Pour poser une question appelant une réponse en OUI/NON, on commence par un auxiliaire (*can, be, have, do, may*...). On emploie le même auxiliaire dans la réponse.

– ***Can*** *you help me please? – Yes, I* ***can****.*

– ***Is*** *she reading? – No, she* ***isn't****.*

– ***Does*** *your father work in Bristol? – Yes, he* ***does****.*

– ***Is there*** *a good film on TV tonight ? – No,* ***there isn't****.*

Dans certains cas, on renforce ou on atténue la réponse par une expression autre que *YES* ou *NO*: *I think, I suppose, I imagine, I hope, Of course*...

– ***Can*** *you play the guitar?*

– ***Of course*** *I can!* (Bien sûr que oui !)

– ***Has*** *she got a good job?*

– ***I hope*** *she has.* (j'espère que oui.)

6 Make sentences.

Écris cinq questions et cinq réponses à l'aide des mots proposés.
Aide-toi de la ponctuation et des majuscules.

1. you / Can / English / Italian? / or / speak / English only / I / can / .

– .... – ....

2. Chinese / Are / Korean? / you / or / I'm / Neither.

– .... – ....

3. rap / prefer / hate / Do / or / rock? / you / I / Neither. / music.

– .... – ....

4. dinner? / pizza / for / fish / or / you / Do / prefer / I'm / I'll have / both. / hungry.

– .... – ....

5. want / ice cream / you / a piece of / some / Do / or / cake? / please / Both.

– .... – ....

MON SCORE | 5

REMEMBER!

OR- QUESTIONS

Dans certaines questions, on propose le **choix entre deux possibilités**.
– Do you prefer maths or English? – Est ce que tu préfères les maths ou l'anglais ?
On peut alors choisir l'une des deux possibilités : *– I prefer maths / English.* – Je préfère les maths / l'Anglais.
On peut choisir les deux possibilités : *– Both.* – Les deux.
On peut refuser les deux possibilités : *– Neither.* – Ni l'un ni l'autre.

7 Translate into English.

MON SCORE | 5

1. Regarde-le ! Il travaille. ....

2. Il doit être en train de travailler. *He must* ....

3. Il se peut qu'il soit en train de travailler. *He may* ....

4. – Travaille-t-il ou regarde-t-il la télévision ? – Ni l'un ni l'autre.

– .... – ....

5. – Est-ce que tu travailles demain? – Oui.

– .... – ....

CALCULE TON TAUX DE RÉUSSITE SUR CE CHAPITRE

Entre 100% et 80%, tu as tout compris. BRAVO !
Entre 80% et 60%, c'est bien.
Si tu as moins de 60%, refais les tests dans quelques jours.

	| 10	1
+	| 5	2
+	| 10	3
+	| 10	4
+	| 5	5
+	| 5	6
+	| 5	7
=	| 50	

x 2 =

% de réussite

GAMES!

DES JEUX !

Find the opposite. Trouve le contraire de chaque mot de la colonne de droite dans la colonne de gauche et relie-les d'un trait comme dans l'exemple.

Always •	• *Boring*
Arrive •	• *Complex*
Attack •	• *Defend*
Be Born •	• *Depart*
Better •	• *Die*
Certitude •	• *Doubt*
Clever •	• *Empty*
Come In •	• *Find*
Cry •	• *Forget*
Far •	• *Future*
First •	• *Go Out*
Full •	• *Happy*
Hard •	• *Last*
High •	• *Later*
Interesting •	• *Laugh*
Land •	• *Low*
Now •	• *Near*
Lose •	• *Never*
Past •	• *Sick*
Remember •	• *Sit Down*
Sad •	• *Soft*
Simple •	• *Stupid*
Stand Up •	• *Take Off*
Thin •	• *Thick*
Well •	• *Worse*

JE FAIS LE POINT...

SPÉCIAL BREVET

OCTOBRE | DÉCEMBRE | FÉVRIER | MARS | JUIN

JE COMPRENDS CE QUE J'ENTENDS

1 J'écoute et je comprends. On me demande : PISTE 6 | 5

1. a. où je suis. / b. qui je suis. / c. comment je vais.
2. a. si j'aime le rugby. / b. si je joue au rugby. / c. si j'aimerais jouer au rugby.
3. a. ce que j'aime faire. / b. ce que je suis en train de faire. / c. ce que fais ici.
4. a. quand je vais aller déjeuner. / b. où je déjeune habituellement. / c. avec qui je déjeune.
5. a. si je dois partir. / b. quand je dois partir. / c. pourquoi je dois partir.

2 Je sais écrire ce que l'on me dicte. PISTE 7

1. ....
2. ....
3. ....
4. ....
5. .... | 5

JE COMPRENDS CE QUE JE LIS

3 Je sais relier logiquement des phrases. | 5

1. *The English usually* ■ ■ *a. there are in New Zealand?*
2. *You can't get in* ■ ■ *b. have tea for breakfast.*
3. *Do you know how many Maoris* ■ ■ *c. Jamaica next weekend?*
4. *It's 8 o'clock.* ■ ■ *d. because it's too early.*
5. *Are you really going to* ■ ■ *e. They must be having breakfast.*

4 Je sais reconnaître de qui on parle.

an actor / a customs-officer / a dentist / a fortune-teller / a journalist / a mechanic / a novelist / a pilot / a taxi-driver / a veterinarian

1. *Captain O'Connor speaking. Welcome on board. The temperature outside is now -34°. Have a pleasant flight.* ....
2. *Open your mouth and stand still. It won't hurt.* ....
3. *Are you sure this hyena gets the food it needs? I doubt vegetables are what it really likes.* ....
4. *Do you sometimes check the oil, Miss? There's a funny noise in the engine.* ....
5. *I can tell you will marry a rich girl. I can see her now in my crystall ball.* ....
6. *Where were you exactly when the gangsters started shooting at the policemen?* ....
7. *London Airport. £35, please. And don't forget your luggage!* ....
8. *To be or not to be.* ....

9. Do you have anything to declare? .... | 10

10. My book is about a young man who falls in love with a girl who hates him. ....

5 Je comprends et je traduis.

1. What time do you have your maths lesson? ....
2. Does he really work in Singapore? ....
3. She may arrive late tonight. ....
4. She thinks I'm too young. ....
5. I can't translate this sentence. ....

| 5

JE COMPRENDS ET J'ÉCRIS

6 Je sais traduire ces phrases.

1. Il pleut souvent. ....
2. Est-ce qu'il pleut souvent ? ....
3. Il ne pleut pas très souvent. ....
4. Regarde ! Il pleut ! ....
5. Le ciel est gris. Il se peut qu'il pleuve. ....

| 5

7 Je sais répondre affirmativement ou négativement.

1. – Is it time for dinner? – No, ...
2. – Am I your best friend? – Yes, ...
3. – Can I ask you another question? – No, ...
4. – Can your sister play the drums? – Yes, ...
5. – Are there any nice boys in your class? – No, ...
6. – Is there a party at Emma's tonight?– Yes, ...
7. – May I come with you? – No, ...
8. – May we take photos, please? – Yes, ...
9. – Do you have a room of your own? – No, ...
10. – Don't you have a mobile phone? – Of course .... !

| 10

8 Je sais joindre la réponse à sa question.

1. How many weeks are there in two years? ■	■ a. 50.
2. How many kilometres are there in 3 miles? ■	■ b. 8.
3. How many states are there in the United States? ■	■ c. 15.
4. How many players are there in a rugby team? ■	■ d. 104.
5. How many planets are there in the solar system? ■	■ e. 4.8

| 5

TOTALISE TES POINTS ET MULIPLIE LE TOTAL PAR 2 POUR OBTENIR TON TAUX DE RÉUSSITE

| 50

x 2 =

% de réussite

Entre 100% et 80%, tu as tout compris. BRAVO !
Entre 80% et 60%, c'est bien.
Si tu as moins de 60%, refais les tests dans quelques jours.

▸ EMPLOI DU PRÉTÉRIT SIMPLE
▸ FORMATION DU PRÉTÉRIT SIMPLE
▸ *WH-QUESTIONS*

unit 3

Who conquered England in 1066?

JE COMPRENDS CE QUE J'ENTENDS

PISTE 8

MON SCORE | 10

1 True or false?

	True	False
1. Carla doesn't like history.		
2. Nick is doing a competition.		
3. He must answer five geography questions.		
4. Elizabeth II became Queen when she was 26.		
5. There were 16 kings or queens between the two Elizabeths.		
6. King George I was born in England.		
7. Admiral Nelson died at the beginning of the 19th century.		
8. Nelson died during the battle of Trafalgar.		
9. Napoleon I invaded England in 1805.		
10. Carla is good at history but isn't very modest.		

REMEMBER!

L'EMPLOI DU PRÉTÉRIT SIMPLE

On emploie le prétérit pour parler d'un événement passé.
Il y a en général dans la phrase un repère temporel explicite, une date, un marqueur : *yesterday, last week, in 1616... I went to Italy in 2007.* Je suis allé en Italie en 2007.
ou sous-entendu : *I went to Italy when I was 20.* Je suis allé en Italie à l'âge de 20 ans.
Le prétérit simple correspond en français
au passé simple : *Shakespeare died in 1616 in Stratford.* Shakespeare mourut en 1616 à Stratford.
au passé composé : *When did you see that film?* Quand as-tu vu ce film ?
à l'imparfait : *He didn't often come when I was ill.* Il ne venait pas souvent quand j'étais malade.
Ago entraîne l'emploi du prétérit simple : *I met your sister three weeks ago.* J'ai rencontré ta sœur il y a trois semaines.

2 Listen and complete.

PISTE 9

MON SCORE | 5

Écoute et complète ces phrases.

1. *Christopher Columbus .... in Genoa in ....*
2. *.................................... it was possible to reach India .... sailing west.*
3. *The King and Queen of Spain .... him three ships to .... to India.*
4. *He .... Spain on 3rd August 1492 and .... America on 12th October 1492.*
5. *He .... in Spain in 1506 but he never .... he had discovered America.*

3 Transform these sentences.

MON SCORE | 5

Transforme ces phrases à la forme suggérée par le contexte.

1. 1. He came last night. → .... last night?
2. We saw you yesterday. → .... didn't ....
3. Tom bought a car last month. → ....?
4. They decided to help him. → .... n't.. .
5. Jessica was born in Spain. → Where ....?

4 True or false?

Vrai ou faux ?

I William, Duke of Normandy

I was born in 1027 in Falaise, Normandy, and my father was Robert II, Duke of Normandy. Of course I became Duke of Normandy when my father died. I was then 7 years old. The French King, Henry I, helped me to take control of Normandy because I had many rivals. I married my cousin Matilda in 1053. She was then 22 and I was 26. We had four sons and six daughters. I became more and more powerful and King Henry tried to invade Normandy in 1054 and 1057 but I resisted and Henry's troops left Normandy. King Edward the Confessor then promised me the throne of England after his death because he had no children. But after Edward's death on January 4th, 1066, Harold Godwinson was crowned King of England as Harold II and, as you can imagine, I was very angry! *(to be continued Unit 4 p. 26)*

	True	False
1. William's father, Robert II died in 1034.		
2. William became Duke of Normandy when he was a child.		
3. The King of France helped William to fight his rivals.		
4. William and Matilda got married when William was 30.		
5. William and Matilda had ten children.		
6. Henry I thought William was becoming too strong.		
7. William said Edward had promised him the throne of England.		
8. King Edward died in 1065.		
9. King Edward's son became King of England.		
10. William was very happy when Harold became King of England.		

MON SCORE | 10

REMEMBER!

FORMATION DU PRÉTÉRIT

LES VERBES RÉGULIERS forment leur prétérit en ajoutant ***–ed*** à la base verbale :
*work → work**ed** / decide → decid**ed** / park → park**ed***
LES VERBES IRRÉGULIERS ont chacun leur formation propre. La **liste** des principaux verbes figure sur le rabat de droite. *buy → **bought** / cut → **cut** / write → **wrote***
Les formes affirmative et négative se forment avec l'auxiliaire *did* et sa négation *didn't*.

I worked	*Did I work?*	*I didn't work*
He, she, it worked	*Did he, she, it work?*	*He, she, it didn't work*
We worked	*Did we work?*	*We didn't work*
You worked	*Did you work?*	*You didn't work*
They worked	*Did they work?*	*They didn't work*

***BE* a deux formes au prétérit :**

I was	*He, she, it was*	*We, you, they were*
I wasn't	*He, she, it wasn't*	*We, you, they weren't*
Was I?	*Was he, she, it?*	*We, you, they weren't*

REMEMBER!

LES -WH QUESTIONS

Ces questions, aussi appelées ouvertes parce que les réponses sont imprévisibles, ont une formation commune : **Wh- + auxiliaire + sujet + verbe + complément ?**
What are you doing upstairs?
Les principaux mots interrogatifs sont : *what, where, when, why, who, whose, which.*
Remarques : Quand un verbe est utilisé avec une **préposition**, celle-ci reste après le verbe :
*What are you waiting **for**?* Qu'est-ce que tu attends ?
Whose, qui est un génitif, reste suivi de l'objet possédé : ***Whose** car was it?* À qui appartenait la voiture ?
Who quand il est **complément** suit la formation habituelle : ***Who** would you like to meet?*
Qui aimerais-tu rencontrer ?
Who quand il est **sujet** entraîne une phrase à la forme affirmative, comme en français d'ailleurs :
***Who** saw you?* Qui t'a vu ?
Which propose un choix limité à des éléments clairement identifiés : ***Which** car do you prefer? The Ferrari or the Porsche?* Quelle voiture préfères-tu ? La Ferrari ou la Porsche ?
What propose un choix général : ***What** car do you like best?* Quelle est la voiture que tu préfères ?
Why (pourquoi) appelle une réponse en ***Because*** : *– **Why** didn't you marry Bruce? – **Because** I didn't love him.* – Pourquoi n'as-tu pas épousé Bruce ? – Parce que je ne l'aimais pas.
What for (pour quoi, dans quel but) appelle une réponse en ***To*** *– **What** did he come **for**? – **To** meet you!*
– Pour quelle raison est-il venu ? – Pour te rencontrer !

5 The right word.

MON SCORE ..... | 10

Choisis le mot interrogatif qui convient en fonction de la réponse.

1. – .... *were you late ? – Because I missed my train.*
2. – .... *actress do you prefer? Meryl Streep or Penelope Cruz?*
3. – .... *was the Great Pyramid of Giza built?*
– About four thousand and five hundred years ago.
4. – .... *children are those? – They're mine. What's wrong with them?*
5. – .... *did you do that for? – To help you.*
6. – .... *are you looking for? – My sister. She must be somewhere in the park.*
7. – .... *'s she like? – She's very good-looking but not too bright.*
8. – .... *didn't you speak to Liza? – Because she pinched my boyfriend last year.*
9. – .... *painted* Rain, Steam and Speed*? – Turner did.*
10. – .... *did you see at Emma's birthday party ? – I saw Sylvia, Claire and Kate.*

6 Translate these sentences.

Traduis ces phrases.

1. Pourquoi n'es-tu pas venu hier ? ....
2. Qui a écrit *L'homme invisible* ? ....
3. Le Titanic a coulé en 1912. ....
4. Est-ce que le film a commencé à trois heures ? ....
5. Qu'as-tu vu quand tu es allé à Londres ? ....

MON SCORE ..... | 5

CALCULE TON TAUX DE RÉUSSITE SUR CE CHAPITRE

Entre 100% et 80%, tu as tout compris. BRAVO !
Entre 80% et 60%, c'est bien.
Si tu as moins de 60%, refais les tests dans quelques jours.

	/10	1
+	/10	2
+	/5	3
+	/10	4
+	/10	5
+	/5	6
=	/50	

x 2 =

% de réussite

GAMES! DES JEUX !

Who am I? **Qui suis-je ?** Chacun des 10 membres de cette famille se présente. Trouve qui parle.

1. My brother and my sister were born on the same day. My name's ______

2. My wife and I had a son and a daughter. My name's ______

3. I've got two brothers. My name's ______

4. I've got two nephews and one niece. My name's ______

5. My husband and I had only one daughter. My name's ______

6. My sister's lucky. She's got two brothers. My name's ______

7. My parents had only one child. My name's ______

8. My sister's got one brother. My name's ______

9. My husband and I had one son and one daughter. My name's ______

10. My wife and I have got one child and three grandchildren. My name's ______

▸ LE PRÉTÉRIT EN *BE+ING*
▸ LE GÉNITIF
▸ LE COMPARATIF

unit 4

What was she doing when you arrived?

JE COMPRENDS CE QUE J'ENTENDS

PISTE 10

MON SCORE | 10

1 Missing words.

Écoute ce texte et ajoute les mots manquants.

It's great to have good friends! I 1. .... some of them last Friday and asked them to come immediately because I 2. .... a big problem. The first one I 3. .... was my old friend Bill. He said he was sorry but he 4. .... dinner with his boss at that moment and couldn't come. Kate was sorry too but she 5. .... with Eddie and it was impossible for her to change her plans. When I phoned Bruce his wife 6. .... me he 7. .... the bathroom and she didn't want to disturb him. Peter and Jane 8. .... bridge with friends and said it was impossible to quit. Tony 9. .... anything special but he was very tired and said he preferred staying at home. Then I phoned my next-door neighbours and they 10. .... immediately. So I wasn't alone to celebrate my birthday !

PISTE 11

2 a, b or c?

Écoute ces cinq phrases et entoure la solution correspondante.

MON SCORE | 5

1. a. Il viendra demain soir. / b. Il vient tous les soirs. / c. Il arrive ce soir.
2. a. Il m'attendra. / b. Il m'attendait. / c. Il m'attend.
3. a. Elle est en train de se marier. / b. Elle va se marier. / c. Elle vient de se marier.
4. a. John a pris ton ordinateur. / b. Il est en train de le prendre. / c. Il va le prendre.
5. a. Elle a rendez-vous avec son nouveau patron. / b. Elle est en train de discuter avec lui. / c. Elle l'a déjà rencontré.

JE COMPRENDS CE QUE JE LIS

REMEMBER!

LE PRÉTÉRIT EN *BE+ING*

Cette forme permet de se replonger dans **une scène du passé**. On décrit ainsi ce qui se passait à un certain moment ou ce que l'on faisait

quand quelque chose s'est passé : *I was having dinner when the phone rang.*
J'étais en train de dîner quand le téléphone a sonné.

pendant que quelque chose d'autre se déroulait : *Some of them were talking while others were dancing.*
Certains d'entre eux parlaient tandis que d'autres dansaient.

Ce prétérit **se forme à l'aide de *WAS, WASN'T*** au singulier et ***WERE, WEREN'T*** au pluriel :

I, he, she, it was singing.	*We, you, they were singing.*
I, he, she, it wasn't singing.	*We, you, they weren't singing.*
Was I, he, she, it singing?	*Were we, you, they singing?*

3 3. Translate these sentences.

Traduis ces phrases.

MON SCORE | 5

1. What were you doing last Monday between 10 and 11 o'clock?

....

2. I think I was working in the garden. ....

3. Are you sure? It was raining hard at that time. ....

4. Oh, yes I remember. I was tidying my garage when Fred Gore rang at the gate.

....

5. Right. A neighbour saw him come in. The problem is he never reappeared...

....

REMEMBER!

LE GÉNITIF

On exprime **la possession** en faisant suivre le possesseur de **'s** et de l'objet possédé :
*David's Jaguar is in Jane**'s** garage.* La jaguar de David est dans le garage de Jane.
Si **le possesseur est au pluriel** on ajoute simplement l'apostrophe :
*Her parents**'** house is quite small.* La maison de ses parents est toute petite.
On peut **sous-entendre l'objet possédé** parce qu'il est évident ou pour éviter une répétition :
*She works at McDonald**'s** (restaurant).* Elle travaille chez McDonald.
*That isn't my bike. It's Bob**'s**.* Ce n'est pas mon vélo. C'est celui de Bob.
Les pronoms possessifs permettent de remplacer l'objet possédé. Ils s'accordent avec le possesseur.
mine le mien, la mienne, les miens, les miennes *ours* le nôtre, la nôtre, les nôtres
yours le tien, la tienne, les tiens, les tiennes, le vôtre, la vôtre, les vôtres
his, hers le sien, la sienne, les siennes (à lui ou à elle) *theirs* la leur, les leurs
This isn't mine. It's yours. Ceci n'est pas à moi. C'est à toi.
Notez l'expression *... of mine. She's a friend of mine.* C'est une amie à moi.
Whose permet de demander qui est le possesseur : *Whose phone is this?* À qui est ce téléphone ?

4 Read and choose.

Lis ces e-mails et choisis la solution qui convient.

From: *smtha.mail@chat.com* ***To:*** *ky.mail@chat.com*
Date: *Sept. 27th* ***Time:*** *10:30 p.m.*
Hi Kitty! R U connected? Have you seen Maggy's new shoes? Her shoes look like mine, don't they?

From: *ky.mail@chat.com* ***To:*** *smtha.mail@chat.com*
Date: *Sept. 27th* ***Time:*** *10:33 p.m.*
Don't worry Samantha. Yours are much nicer. And personally I hate her jeans. Who wears red jeans? She pretends she saw them in Cosmogirl. I can't believe it…By the way whose mobile did you use yesterday? Have you bought a new one or was it someone else's?

From: *smtha.mail@chat.com* ***To:*** *ky.mail@chat.com*
Date: *Sept. 27th* ***Time:*** *10:35 p.m.*
It was Alan's… I'll tell you later. See U. XXXXX

From: *ky.mail@chat.com* ***To:*** *smtha.mail@chat.com*
Date: *Sept. 27th* ***Time:*** *10:38 p.m.*
Don't tell me! It's Alan Stilwell! That boy is crazy!

From: *smtha.mail@chat.com* ***To:*** *ky.mail@chat.com*
Date: *Sept. 27th* ***Time:*** *10:39 p.m.*
It is Alan Stilwell. And he isn't crazy. He's cute. R U jealous?

1. a. Maggy and Samantha / b. Samatha and Alan / c. Samantha and Kitty are chatting.
2. p.m means a. in the morning / b. in the evening / c. the following day.
3. Maggy has a. new shoes / b. a new phone / c. a new boyfriend.
4. Cosmogirl is a. a film / b. a shop / c. a magazine.
5. Samantha phoned a. Alan / b. Kitty / c. Maggy yesterday.
6. She used a. Alan's phone / b. her own phone / c. Kitty's phone.
7. You say See you when a. you like / b. you meet / c. you leave someone.
8. Samantha a. likes Alan / b. hates Alan / c. thinks Alan is crazy.
9. a. Alan is jealous / b. Samantha thinks Alan is cute. / c. Maggy doesn't like Alan.
10. Samantha thinks a. Kitty likes Alan / b. Kitty is jealous. / c. Alan likes Kitty.

MON SCORE ..... | 10

JE SAIS M'EXPRIMER

REMEMBER!

LE COMPARATIF

Quand on compare deux éléments on prend le second comme repère.
Le premier élément peut être égal au second. On utilise ***as ... as*** : *Ann is **as** nice and intelligent **as** John.* Ann est aussi gentille et aussi intelligente que John.
Le premier élément peut être supérieur au second. **L'adjectif court** (une ou deux syllabes) est suivi de *-er than* : *John is tall**er than** me.* John est plus grand que moi.
L'adjectif long (plus de deux syllabes) est précédé de ***more*** : *I'm **more** intelligent **than** John.* Je suis plus intelligent que John.
Le premier élément peut être inférieur au second. On utilise ***less ... than*** : *The book is **less** interesting **than** the film.* Le livre est moins intéressant que le film.
Certains comparatifs sont irréguliers : *good/better :* bon/meilleur *bad/worse :* mauvais/pire

5 Make sentences.

Compare ces éléments à l'aide des mots fournis. Les symboles =, +, – correspondent à égalité, supériorité et infériorité.

MON SCORE ..... | 5

1. + big → an elephant / a hippopotamus ....
2. = good → tea / coffee ....
3. + expensive → a car / a motorbike ....
4. – intelligent → my sister / you ....
5. = dangerous → a snake / a scorpion ....

6 Translate these sentences.

Traduis ces phrases.

1. La famille de ma femme est australienne. ....
2. À qui sont ces chaussures ? .... ?
3. Ce sont celles d'Emma. Celles de Clémentine sont roses. ....
4. Les deux fils des Wilson vivent à Londres. ....
5. La voiture de Frank est anglaise. La mienne est japonaise.

....

MON SCORE ..... | 5

CALCULE TON TAUX DE RÉUSSITE SUR CE CHAPITRE

Entre 100% et 80%, tu as tout compris. BRAVO !
Entre 80% et 60%, c'est bien.
Si tu as moins de 60%, refais les tests dans quelques jours.

	... / 10	1
+	... / 5	2
+	... / 5	3
+	... / 10	4
+	... / 5	5
+	... / 5	6
+	... / 10	7
=	... / 50	

x 2 =

... % de réussite

7 Complete these sentences.

MON SCORE ... / 10

Utilise les 10 propositions suivantes pour compléter ces phrases.
danced / didn't work / mine / than / that / was dancing / wasn't working / Who's / Whose / yours

1. Everyone .... when I left the party.
2. This isn't my phone. .... is pink.
3. We .... all night at Samantha's birthday part
4. Is this phone ....
5. Are you sure .... you can drive a lorry?
6. That Jaguar is much bigger .... your Mini Cooper. Drive carefully.
7. He .... when I left him.
8. .... shoes were they?
9. .... wearing my shoes?
10. He .... last weekend. He said he was too t

GAMES! DES JEUX !

A quiz. Special girls but boys can read it too!
What sort of best friend are you?

1. You're talking with friends after school when one of the girls starts commenting about the ridiculous clothes your best friend wears.
a. You don't say anything but you don't laugh.
b. You laugh with them.
c. You tell her to have a look at her own clothes before talking.

2. Your best friend has a monstrous dog she always goes out with.
a. You refuse to go out with her if she comes along with her dog.
b. You kick the dog when your friend can't see you.
c. You pretend you like the dog.

3. You're out shopping and your friend tries on an orange and purple T-shirt.
a. You tell her you wouldn't like to be with her when she wears it.
b. You tell her to buy it.
c. You say it's fantastic but it doesn't go with her hair.

4. You have said something unpleasant to your friend and she hasn't spoken to you for several days.
a. You just wait for her to speak to you again.
b. You go out with another friend.
c. You send her a message to say you're very sorry.

5. She seems to be interested in your boyfriend.
a. You tell her you'll never forgive her if she goes out with your boyfriend.
b. You go out with her boyfriend.
c. You try to convince her not to spoil your friendship for a boy.

6. You offered her beautiful earrings for her birthday but she doesn't wear them.
a. You don't say anything but you aren't pleased at all.
b. You tell her she'll never get anything else from you.
c. You offer to change them for something else if she doesn't like them.

You got mostly a's.
You're just friends, that's all.

You got mostly b's.
Are you sure that girl is your friend? We'd like to know what you do with your worst enemies!

You got mostly C's.
You are a great best friend. Congratulations!

JE FAIS LE POINT...

DÉCEMBRE

SPÉCIAL BREVET

JE COMPRENDS CE QUE J'ENTENDS

1 J'écoute et j'écris ce que l'on me dit. PISTE 12 | ... / 5

1. ....
2. ....
3. ....
4. ....
5. ....

2 J'écoute et je choisis la bonne réponse. PISTE 13 | ... / 5

1. a. In 1492. / b. 15 years ago. / c. At a hospital. / d. Yes, I was.
2. a. Shakespeare did. / b. Yes, he did. / c. In 1597. / d. A long time ago.
3. a. No, I didn't. / b. Yes, I did. / c. I saw your children. / d. Last night.
4. a. He painted. / b. Yes, he was. / c. He's painting. / d. He was painting.
5. a. Yes, it was. / b. No, I didn't. / c. Yes, it did. / d. Why not?

JE COMPRENDS CE QUE JE LIS

3 Je sais quelle forme verbale employer. | ... / 5

1. It a. rained / b. was raining when I arrived in London.
2. Who a. was telling / b. told them I couldn't come?
3. They a. were sleeping / b. slept when the tsunami hit the island.
4. It a. snowed / b. was snowing for several days in June.
5. What time was it when she a. was falling / b. fell out of the window?

4 Je comprends et je traduis. | ... / 5

1. No one found the solution. ....
2. Your sister is worse than you. ....
3. What did he look like? ....
4. What happened after dinner? ....
5. Whose hat is that? ....

5 Je sais quel verbe irrégulier choisir.

1. I cooked the meal and John a. brought / b. broke the wine.
2. I a. bought / b. brought this T-shirt for £5.
3. What time did your plane a. make / b. take off?
4. Why didn't you a. spend / b. send me a postcard from Canada?
5. I a. rode / b. read a horse for the first time yesterday.

6. I was so angry that I a. hit / b. hid him on the head with a big dictionary.
7. He a. taught / b. thought I wouldn't understand but I did.
8. Everybody admired the dress she a. bore / b. wore that day.
9. The car a. lost / b. cost a lot because it was new.
10. She a. fell / b. felt in love with a man she met on a plane.

| 10

JE COMPRENDS ET J'ÉCRIS

6 Je sais mettre ces mots dans l'ordre.

| 5

1. Julius Caesar / Britain / in / invaded / before / 54 / Christ / and / 55 /
....
2. 12 / what / to / Dickens / happened / Charles / when / was / he / ?
....
3. didn't / wasn't / I / George I / English / know / that /
....
4. reigned / from / Queen / to / 1837 / 1901 / Victoria /
....
5. 1789 / became / George / the / of / the / president / Washington / in / USA / first /
....

7 Je sais traduire ces phrases.

| 5

1. À qui est cette voiture? ....
2. C'est la mienne. ....
3. Je croyais que c'était celle de Claire. ....
4. La voiture de Claire est plus petite que la mienne. ....
5. Mais elle est plus rapide. ....

8 Je sais passer de la forme affirmative à la forme interrogative.

| 5

1. He came yesterday . ...
2. They wrote me a letter. ....
3. Jim understood my question. ....
4. I drank your coffee. ....
5. I went to London in July. ....

9 Je sais passer de la forme interrogative à la forme affirmative.

| 5

1. Did it rain yesterday? ....
2. Was he working between 5 and 6? ....
3. Did the police catch him? ....
4. Did they all get killed? ....
5. Did the accident happen at night? ....

TOTALISE TES POINTS ET MULIPLIE LE TOTAL PAR 2 POUR OBTENIR TON TAUX DE RÉUSSITE

| 50

x 2 =

% de réussite

Entre 100% et 80%, tu as tout compris. BRAVO !
Entre 80% et 60%, c'est bien.
Si tu as moins de 60%, refais les tests dans quelques jours.

▸ L'EXPRESSION DU FUTUR
▸ LE SUPERLATIF
▸ *SOME, ANY, NO*

5 unit

What will you do when you grow up?

JE COMPRENDS CE QUE J'ENTENDS

PISTE 14

1 True or false?

Écoute cette conversation et dis si ces affirmations sont vraies ou fausses.

	True	False
1. Steve is pleased to meet Rebecca.		
2. Rebecca has a plan for next weekend.		
3. Steve's sister is arriving from Canada tonight.		
4. Jane's husband's name is Scott.		
5. Scott is interested in history.		
6. Steve wants to go to Stonehenge with his friends this Saturday.		
7. Rebecca is sure that Steve and Jane would like to go tc Stonehenge.		
8. Jane prefers shopping to visiting places of historical interest.		
9. Rebecca will go to Stonehenge with Steve.		
10. Rebecca asks Steve to go to the airport with her.		

MON SCORE ... /10

REMEMBER!

L'EXPRESSION DU FUTUR

Le futur s'exprime essentiellement de quatre façons en anglais :

- le plus souvent, à l'aide du **modal *will / won't*** *What will you do when you grow up?* Que feras-tu quand tu seras grand ? *I won't work in an office.* Je ne travaillerai pas dans un bureau.
- à l'aide de la locution ***be going to*** pour exprimer une intention ou une prévision *They're going to get married.* Ils vont se marier. *Isn't it going to snow?* Est-ce qu'il ne va pas neiger ?
- par l'emploi du **présent en *be+ing* avec un indicateur de temps** *They're arriving tomorrow morning.* Ils arrivent demain matin.
- par l'emploi du **présent simple pour un horaire ou un emploi du temps** *My plane takes off at 2 o'clock and lands at 6.* Mon avion décolle à 2h et atterrit à 6h.

PISTE 15

2 Listen and complete these sentences.

Complète ces phrases.

1. .... *a double cheeseburger and a big coke, please.*

2. .... *with that revolver?*

3. Hurry up! .... *at 8 o'clock.*

4. .... *a new computer?*

5. – .... *Jane? – No, I* ....

MON SCORE ... /5

3 True or false?

Vrai ou faux ?

I William the Conqueror, King of England

I asked Pope Alexander II to declare I was the legitimate king, which he did. I assembled an army and promised lands to the men who would help me. I was lucky because King Harald III of Norway attacked Harold in the North of England. He also wanted to be King of England! I landed with my 600 ships and 7,000 soldiers at Pevensey, on the south coast of England on September 25th, 1066. I moved to Hastings and built a wooden castle as a base for the battles to come. Meanwhile Harold defeated the King of Norway on September 28th but he lost lots of soldiers in the battle. He arrived on October 13th and the big battle took place the next day. At the beginning Edward's troops were stronger than mine but I was cleverer and when Harold was killed by an arrow in the eye my victory was complete. I decided then to go to London and the Saxon noblemen, exhausted by long battles, acclaimed me and I became King of England on Christmas Day 1066 in Westminster Abbey. Unfortunately I had to fight my enemies for years and years and I died in a battle in September 1087 when I fell off my horse!

	True	False
1. The Pope said Harold was the legitimate King of England.		
2. William assembled an army to invade Norway.		
3. The King of Norway wanted to become King of England.		
4. Harald III was defeated by the King of England on September 28th.		
5. William had 6,000 ships and 7,000 soldiers.		
6. Pevensey is located in the north of England.		
7. The battle took place on October 14th.		
8. King Harold was killed during the battle.		
9. William became King of England on November 25th.		
10. William died at he age of 60.		

MON SCORE |10

REMEMBER!

LE SUPERLATIF

Le superlatif permet de désigner un élément comme étant « le plus » ou « le moins ».

« Le plus » On ajoute ***the* + *–est*** à un **adjectif court** (une ou deux syllabes) ***the nicest** boy in the class* le garçon le plus gentil de la classe

ou l'on fait précéder un **adjectif long** (plus de deux syllabes) de ***the most***

***the most** interesting film of the week* le film le plus intéressant de la semaine

« Le moins » On utilise ***the least*** ***the least** expensive book in the shop* le livre le moins cher de la boutique

Certains adjectifs ont une forme irrégulière. *good → the best :* bon → le meilleur/le mieux

bad → the worst : mauvais → le pire

4 a, b or c?

Choisis la bonne solution.

1. The United States' first president was *a. Georges W. Bush / b. Arnold Schwarzenegger / c. Georges Washington.*
2. The United States' largest state is *a. Alaska / b. California / c. New Jersey.*
3. Australia's most famous animals are *a. mice / b. rabbits / c. kangaroos.*
4. Canada's most populated town is *a. Vancouver / b. Toronto / c. Montreal.*

MON SCORE |10

5. The highest mountain in the world is a. Mount Everest / b. Mont Blanc / c. Mount Snowdon.
6. The Sun's smallest planet is a. Earth / b. Mercury / c. Mars.
7. The most distant galaxy from earth is a. NGC 4144 / b. Abell 1835 IR1916 / c. The Milky Way.
8. The most spoken language is a. Mandarin / b. Spanish / c. English.
9. The earliest known bird is a. the archaeopteryx / b. the ostrich / c. the flamingo.
10. The tallest tree in the world is a. 106 metres / b. 115 metres / c. 48 metres tall.

JE SAIS M'EXPRIMER

REMEMBER!

SOME, ANY, NO

Some s'emploie pour parler d'une certaine **quantité non précisée**. *I'll meet **some** old friends tomorrow.* Je vais rencontrer quelques vieux amis demain. *There's **some** coffee left.* Il reste du café.
Dans les questions, on emploie *some* quand on est **sûr d'avoir une réponse positive**.
*Can I have **some** tea?* Est-ce que je peux avoir du thé ?
Sinon, on emploie ***any***. *Is there **any** coffee left?* Est-ce qu'il reste du café ? *Do you have **any** problems?* As-tu des problèmes ?
Any **peut signifier « n'importe lequel »**. *Take **any** book.* Prends n'importe quel livre.
No / Not any **s'emploient pour la forme négative**. *There's **no** coffee / **not any** coffee left.* Il ne reste pas de café. *I have **no** friends / I **don't** have **any** friends.* Je n'ai pas d'amis.
Some, any et ***no*** s'associent **avec *one / body / thing / where*** : *someone/somebody :* quelqu'un *no one/nobody :* personne *anyone/anybody :* n'importe qui *something :* quelque chose *nothing :* rien *anything :* n'importe quoi *somewhere :* quelque part *nowhere :* nulle part *anywhere :* n'importe où

5 Some, any ou no?

MON SCORE | /10

Complète ces phrases par *some*, *any* ou *no* selon le sens.

1. Is there .... coke in the fridge?
2. I'd like .... tea, please. I'm thirsty.
3. May I take .... cakes, Mum?
4. There's .... petrol in the car. It won't start!
5. I haven't got .... thing to read. Can I take that book, please?
6. Listen! There's .... one in the house!
7. I can't find my shoes .... where. Do you know where they are?
8. Don't you think there's .... thing strange in what she says?
9. .... body loves me! I'm very unhappy!
10. I didn't find .... interesting people at her party.

6 Translate these sentences.

MON SCORE | /5

Traduis ces phrases.

1. Quand viendras-tu me voir ? ....
2. Est-ce que tu vas acheter l'ordinateur le plus cher du magasin ?
....
3. Il ne reste personne dans la maison. ....
4. Jane est la meilleure élève de sa classe. ....
5. Je pars demain matin. ....

CALCULE TON TAUX DE RÉUSSITE SUR CE CHAPITRE

Entre 100% et 80%, tu as tout compris. BRAVO !
Entre 80% et 60%, c'est bien.
Si tu as moins de 60%, refais les tests dans quelques jours.

	/10	1
+	/5	2
+	/10	3
+	/10	4
+	/10	5
+	/5	6
=	/50	

x 2 =

% de réussite

GAMES! DES JEUX !

They have something in common.
Trouve ce que ces couples de personnages célèbres ont en commun.

1. Ludwig van Beethoven and Thomas Edison.
a. Both of them had seven sons.
b. They both became deaf very young.
c. They both composed music.

2. Shakespeare and Molière.
a. They were both actors and playwrights.
b. They both died on stage.
c. They both travelled to Italy and Spain.

3. Abraham Lincoln and John Fitzgerald Kennedy.
a. They both lived in California.
b. Both of them were representatives for Illinois.
c. Both of them were assassinated.

4. Queen Elizabeth I and Queen Elizabeth II.
a. They both had problems with their children.
b. They both reigned for more than forty years.
c. Both their mothers were executed.

5. Isaac Newton and Albert Einstein.
a. They were both English.
b. They developed the use of telescopes.
c. They both proposed theories of the universe.

6. Julius Caesar and Napoleon I.
a. They were both assassinated.
b. They both invaded England.
c. Only one of them invaded England.

7. Charles Dickens and Mark Twain.
a. Young boys were the heroes of several of their novels.
b. They both went to prison.
c. They both took pen names to write their books.

8. Bill Gates and Steve Jobs.
a. Both of them were born in 1955.
b. They are both very poor.
c. They both designed computers.

9. Rosa Parks and Irene Morgan.
a. They were both movie stars.
b. Both wrote novels.
c. They both refused to give their seats to white people in buses.

10. Charlie Chaplin and Alfred Hitchcock.
a. They were both married four times.
b. They were both English.
c. Both of them had to leave the USA for political reasons.

▸ FORMATION DU *PRESENT PERFECT*
▸ EMPLOI DU *PRESENT PERFECT*
▸ LES *HOW-QUESTIONS*

unit 6

I've been waiting for you for hours!

JE COMPRENDS CE QUE J'ENTENDS

PISTE 16

1 True or false?

Vrai ou faux ?

MON SCORE /10

	True	False
1. This conversation takes place in a café.		
2. Sean has been waiting for Laura for 10 minutes.		
3. Laura says she is late because she was with Gordon.		
4. Sean doesn't like Gordon.		
5. Gordon is Laura's ex-boyfriend.		
6. In fact Laura didn't see Gordon.		
7. She wanted to be sure Sean was in love with her.		
8. Laura is disappointed with Sean.		
9. Sean is angry with Laura.		
10. The story has a happy ending.		

REMEMBER!

FORMATION DU *PRESENT PERFECT*

Le *present perfect* simple se forme avec le présent de l'auxiliaire *HAVE* suivi du participe passé du verbe conjugué. *I have worked well.* J'ai bien travaillé.

Rappel : Le participe passé d'un verbe régulier se forme avec la base verbale + ***-ed*** : *play :* jouer *played :* joué *finish :* finir *finished :* fini

*I've, you've, we've, they've work**ed***	*Have I, you, we, they work**ed**?*	*I, you, we, they haven't work**ed***
*He, she, it's work**ed***	*Has he, she, it work**ed**?*	*He, she, it hasn't work**ed***

Rappel : Le participe passé d'un verbe irrégulier a une formation qui lui est propre. C'est le 3e terme de la liste sur le rabat de droite de ce livre. *see saw **seen** sing sang **sung***

*I, you, we, they've **sung***	*Have I, you, we, they **sung**?*	*I, you, we, they haven't **sung**.*
*He, she, it's **sung***	*Has he, she, it **sung**?*	*He, she, it hasn't **sung***

Le *present perfect* en *be+ing* se forme avec le présent de l'auxiliare *HAVE* suivi de *BEEN* + *-ing*.
I have been playing for half an hour. Je joue depuis une demi-heure.

PISTE 17

2 Listen and complete.

Écoute et complète ces phrases.

1. *I .... your car. It's clean now.*
2. .... *your brother* .... Harry Potter and the Goblet of Fire?
3. *I' .... just .... your girlfriend.*
4. *Chris .... for three hours.*
5. *How long .... for me?*

MON SCORE /5

JE COMPRENDS CE QUE JE LIS

REMEMBER!

EMPLOI DU *PRESENT PERFECT*

Il s'emploie pour **constater le résultat présent d'un événement passé** :
I've lost my key. I can't open the door. J'ai perdu ma clé. Je ne peux pas ouvrir la porte.
Il faut bien distinguer son emploi de celui du prétérit simple qui, lui, permet de retourner dans le passé (→ la semaine dernière) : *– **Have you seen** that film? – Yes, I have. I **saw** it last week.*
– As-tu vu ce film ? – Oui. Je l'ai vu la semaine dernière.
Il s'emploie aussi pour **décrire une action commencée dans le passé et qui dure encore**.
On indique **le point de départ avec *since* + date**, (« depuis »), ou **la durée avec *for* + durée**. Le verbe est alors au présent en français. *I have known Laura **since** Christmas.* Je connais Laura depuis Noël.
*I have known Laura **for** six months.* { Je connais Laura depuis six mois. / OU Il y a six mois que je connais Laura.
Le *present perfect* s'emploie aussi avec ***have* + *be+ing***. *I have been painting my room.* J'ai peint ma chambre. (J'ai de la peinture sur les mains...) *I have painted my room.* J'ai peint ma chambre. (Voyez le résultat.)

3 Translate these sentences.

MON SCORE | 5

Traduis ces phrases.

1. *Have you done your homework?* ....
2. *She's lived in London for two weeks.* ....
3. *She's been trying to stop smoking since Christmas.* ....
4. *We've been working for hours!* ....
5. *They have found the murderer.* ....

4 a or b?

Choisis le temps qui convient à chaque phrase.

1. *Look! I a. have bought / b. bought a fantastic T-shirt. Do you like it?*
2. *I a. have lost / b. lost my phone last night.*
3. *I a. have been working / b. was working for two hours. I'm tired.*
4. *What a. have you been doing / b. were you doing when I arrived?*
5. *a. He's changed / b. He changed since he got married.*
6. *I a. have bought / b. bought a new racket. I'm going to win the championship.*
7. *a. I didn't see / b. I haven't seen* Star Wars 7 *last week. What was it like?*
8. *They a. were married / b. have been married since Christmas.*
9. *– How long a. have you known / b. did you know her ? – Six weeks.*
10. *We a. visited / b. have visited Hollywood in 2007.*

MON SCORE | 10

5 The right order.

Mets ces phrases dans le bon ordre.

1. *When the Spanish arrived, the Mayas abandoned their temple.*
2. *Mr Yuriko has refused to say where the temple is situated to protect it from any "visitors".*
3. *A Japanese explorer, Kenji Yuriko, has discovered a temple in Central America.*
4. *No one has seen that temple since then.*
5. *He thinks the Mayas built it seven or eight hundred years ago.*

MON SCORE | 5

100% de réussite en anglais

Claude Gosset

CORRIGÉS DES EXERCICES

3e

ÉDITIONS OPHRYS

graphisme céline farez _ virginie rio

UNIT 1 *DO YOU LIKE SUSHI?*

Page 5

1 PISTE 2

– Oh, hello. I'm your next-door neighbour. You're new here, aren't you?
– Yes, I am. My name's Andy. Andy Penton.
– I'm Patty McLuhan. Welcome to Manchester.
– Thanks. It's quite a change for me. I'm from Vancouver.
– Vancouver! Oh, so you're from Canada, Andy.
– Yes, I am. I'm here because of my father's job.
– What does he do?
– He has a funny job. He's a video game developer.
– Do you mean he makes video games?
– That's it. He works with a team of artists and computer programmers here in Manchester.
– That's a great job! Does your mother work with him?
– No, she doesn't. She's a cook. Do you like sushi?
– Sushi? That's Japanese, isn't it?
– Right. My mother's from Tokyo and she works in a restaurant.
– It wouldn't be that big Japanese restaurant in Liverpool Street, would it?
– That's it. And I work there as a waiter on Saturdays.
– Do they have waitresses, too?
– No, they don't but I can ask Mum if you're interested!
– Great! See you Andy!
– Bye, Patty!

1. True
2. False
3. False
4. False
5. True
6. True
7. True
8. False
9. False
10. True

2 PISTE 3

1. School starts next Monday at 9:30.
2. How often do you repair your motobike?
3. I don't know how many children they have.
4. I don't like watching television. I prefer surfing the net.
5. Great Britain consists of England, Scotland and Wales.

Page 6

3

1. Elle était en colère après moi.
2. Est-ce qu'ils étaient encore en train de danser à minuit ?
3. Le texte est-il traduit en français ?
4. Elle a 17 ans, n'est-ce pas ?
5. Il fait froid aujourd'hui.

4

1. the environment
2. greenhouse effect
3. carbon dioxide
4. photosynthesis
5. the ozone layer

5

1. c
2. a
3. b
4. b
5. c
6. b
7. c
8. c
9. b
10. a

Page 7

6

1. I have a maths lesson every day.
2. He doesn't often come.
3. How many brothers do you have / have you got?
4. How many seconds are there in a week?
5. Where do you have lunch on Mondays?

7

1. is
2. am
3. have
4. had
5. be

Page 8

8

1. I'm not interested in giraffes.
2. There are tigers in China.
3. My sister was at home last night at 11.
4. She doesn't work in a bank.
5. My doctor smokes.

GAMES

A	R	T	F	T	E	T	H	A	N	K	S	A	L	O	T	R	G							
W	E	L	C	O	M	E	T	O	E	N	G	L	A	N	D	N	S							
H	R	T	Y	Y	H	A	V	E	A	N	I	C	E	D	A	Y	X							
W	H	E	R	E	A	R	E	Y	O	U	F	R	O	M	G	G	H							
T	H	E	J	E	W	O	I	M	S	O	R	R	Y	M	A	L	T							
P	L	E	A	S	E	D	T	O	M	E	E	T	Y	O	U	I	A							
A	U	C	L	A	H	O	W	O	L	D	A	R	E	Y	O	U	I							
N	E	N	J	O	Y	Y	O	U	R	S	E	L	F	A	M	I	P							
C	A	N	Y	O	U	R	E	P	E	A	T	P	L	E	A	S	E	H	A	T	I	S	C	V
L	E	N	D	M	E	Y	O	C	A	N	I	H	E	L	P	Y	O	U	P	E	N	S	O	T
A	Q	W	S	P	E	L	L	Y	O	U	R	N	A	M	E	Z	S	X	E	F	V	R	F	B
T	P	I	R	E	R	Y	O	U	C	A	N	T	S	M	O	K	E	H	E	R	E	B	G	C
G	F	W	H	A	T	S	Y	O	U	R	P	H	O	N	E	N	U	M	B	E	R	T	H	J
H	V	H	J	Y	C	A	N	I	S	E	E	Y	O	U	R	P	A	S	S	P	O	R	T	J
B	N	O	P	A	R	K	I	N	G	B	N	J	K	I	U	Y	T	R	A	S	X	C	V	B
G	F	H	U	I	R	T	W	H	A	T	A	B	O	U	T	A	D	R	I	N	K	S	P	H
A	R	E	Y	O	U	O	K	N	A	P	O	L	E	O	W	E	L	L	I	G	T	O	O	N
C	A	E	R	T	T	E	A	O	R	C	O	F	F	E	E	N	E	L	D	S	O	G	B	N
G	O	O	D	M	O	R	N	I	N	G	A	Z	E	R	T	Y	U	I	I	O	P	M	K	G
Q	S	D	F	W	H	A	T	S	Y	O	U	R	J	O	B	S	D	G	H	J	K	T	I	M
W	I	L	D	I	A	S	H	A	S	E	E	Y	O	U	L	A	T	E	R	K	E	S	P	O
C	H	A	R	I	D	O	N	T	U	N	D	E	R	S	T	A	N	D	D	I	C	J	K	E
S	U	P	E	R	T	H	I	N	A	P	M	R	C	V	H	O	W	D	O	Y	O	U	D	O
T	E	R	V	I	C	T	O	R	D	O	N	O	T	D	I	S	T	U	R	B	N	E	M	O

UNIT 2 *WHY AREN'T YOU WORKING?*

▶ Page 9

1 PISTE 4

Mike: Hello, Anne. What do you want? I'm busy.
Anne: Oh, am I disturbing you, Mike?
Mike: No, of course you aren't. I'm very sorry, Anne, but... I'm cooking.
Anne: You're what?
Mike: You heard. I'm cooking. No sexist remarks please.
Anne: Oh, no. That's great. What exactly are you making?
Mike: I'm trying to make a pizza for eleven people.
Anne: Wow! Are you having a party tonight?
Mike : Exactly. I'm inviting all the boys in my football team to celebrate our victory.
Anne: What about buying pizzas?
Mike: I can't. Our rules are very strict. We must cook ourselves.
Anne: I see... No girls of course.
Mike: No girls.
Anne: You know, Mike, I'm a great pizzaiolo.
Mike: That's nice but you can't come. Except if you cook and go home before they arrive.
Anne: You're joking! Eleven boys for one girl and I can't stay!
Mike: The boys may like a change, after all... OK. You're invited. Hurry up!
Anne: Thanks Mike. I'm coming ! (click) Wow! Eleven boys and me!

1. False
2. True
3. True
4. False
5. False
6. True
7. False
8. True
9. True
10. False

2 PISTE 5

1. Queen Elizabeth is going to Balmoral this weekend.
2. Your panther's lying on my coat!
3. The All Blacks are leaving for Europe tomorrow.
4. They aren't coming to my party tonight.
5. What are you talking about?

▶ Page 10

3

1. True	6. True
2. True	7. True
3. False	8. True
4. False	9. True
5. True	10. True

4

1. Les chats ne savent pas nager et les chiens ne savent pas grimper aux arbres.
2. Personne ne répond au téléphone. Ils doivent être sortis.
3. Est-ce que je peux avoir du café, s'il vous plaît ?
4. J'en ai marre ! je ne peux rien faire dans cette maison !
5. Regarde cet homme là-bas. Est-ce que crois que ce peut être un des X-men ?
6. No, tu ne dois pas te servir de la voiture de ton père. Tu n'as pas assez de pratique.
7. Je ne peux pas t'emmener à la discothèque ce soir. Je n'ai pas assez d'argent.
8. Harry et Hermione ! Il vous faut apprendre à vous servir correctement de vos baguettes magiques.
9. Un kangourou roux peut sauter à trois mètres de hauteur.
10. Il a téléphoné il y a dix minutes. Il se peut qu'il soit en retard.

▶ Page 11

5

1. Yes, he is.	4. Of course I do
2. No, there aren't.	5. Yes, you may.
3. Yes, you can.	

6

1. – Can you speak English or Italian ?
– I can only speak English.
2. – Are you Chinese or Korean ?
– I'm neither.
3. – Do you prefer rap or rock?
– Neither. I hate music.
4. – Do you prefer pizza or fish for dinner?
– I'll have both. I'm hungry.
5. – Do you want ice cream or a piece of cake?
– Both, please.

▶ Page 12

7

1. Look at him! He's working.
2. He must be working.
3. He may be working.
4. Is he working or watching television? Neither.
5. Are you working tomorrow? Yes, I am.

GAMES

Always → Never	Clever → Stupid
Arrive → Depart	Come In → Go Out
Attack → Defend	Cry → Laugh
Be Born → Die	Far → Near
Better → Worse	First → Last
Certitude → Doubt	Full → Empty
Hard → Soft	Past → Future
High → Low	Remember → Forget
Interesting → Boring	
Land → Take Off	Sad → Happy
Lose → Find	Simple → Complex
Now → Later	Stand Up → Sit Down
Thin → Thick	Well → Sick

JE FAIS LE POINT OCTOBRE

▶ Page 13

1 PISTE 6

1. c. How are you?
2. a. Do you like rugby?
3. b. What are you doing at the moment?
4. b. Where do you have lunch?
5. c. Why must you go now?

2 PISTE 7

1. How many sisters do you have?
2. Where are you from?
3. What do you do after school?
4. Can you drive a car?
5. What's your brother doing at the moment?

JE FAIS LE POINT OCTOBRE

3
1. b
2. d
3. a
4. e
5. c

4
1. a pilot
2. a dentist
3. a veterinarian / a vet
4. a mechanic
5. a fortune-teller
6. a journalist
7. a taxi-driver
8. an actor
9. a customs-officer
10. a novelist

▶ Page 14

5
1. À quelle heure as-tu un cours de maths ?
2. Est-ce qu'il travaille vraiment à Singapour ?
3. Il se peut qu'elle arrive tard ce soir.
4. Elle pense que je suis trop jeune.
5. Je ne sais pas traduire cette phrase.

6
1. It often rains.
2. Does it often rain?
3. It doesn't often rain.
4. Look! It's raining.
5. The sky is grey. It may rain.

7
1. No, it isn't.
2. Yes, you are.
3. No, you can't.
4. Yes, she can.
5. No, there aren't.
6. Yes there is.
7. No, you may not
8. Yes, you may
9. No, I don't.
10. Of course I do!

8
1. d. 104
2. e. 4.8
3. a. 50
4. c. 15
5. b. 8

UNIT 3 *WHO CONQUERED ENGLAND IN 1066?*

▶ Page 15

1 PISTE 8

Nick: *Hi, Carla. I'm pleased to see you. Are you good at history?*
Carla: *Well, Nick, I'm interested in history. Do you want me to help you?*
Nicky: *Yes, please. I'm doing a competition in a history magazine. There are five questions.*
Carla: *OK.*
Nicky: *First question. Who became Queen of England at the age of 26? Elizabeth I, Victoria or Elizabeth II?*
Carla: *Quite simple. It was Elizabeth II.*
Nick: *Great. Second question. How many kings or queens were there in England between Elizabeth I and Elizabeth II? Twelve, sixteen or eighteen?*
Carla: *Let me think... Sixteen.*
Nick: *Wow! Third question: Where was King George I from? Germany, Italy or Scotland.*
Carla: *Simple. He was German.*
Nick: *Thanks. Fourth question: What happened to Admiral Nelson in 1805? He won the battle of Trafalgar, he died or he got married.*
Carla: *He won the battle and he died.*
Nic: *Are you sure?*
Carla: *Of course I am!*
Nick: *OK. Last question: Who did not invade England? Napoleon I, Julius Caesar or William I?*
Carla: *I don't know.*
Nick: *What?... OK, Carla. So Napoleon I, Julius Caesar or William I?*
Carla: *Napoleon I.*
Nick: *Thanks, Carla. You're the best.*
Carla: *I know.*

1. False
2. True
3. False
4. True
5. True
6. False
7. True
8. True
9. False
10. True

2 PISTE 9

1. Christopher Columbus was born in Genoa in 1451.
2. He thought it was possible to reach India by sailing west.
3. The King and Queen of Spain gave him three ships to sail to India.
4. He left Spain on 3rd August 1492 and discovered America on 12th October 1492.
5. He died in Spain in 1506 but he never knew he had discovered America.

▶ Page 16

3

1. Did he come last night?
2. We didn't see you yesterday.
3. Did Tom buy a car last month?
4. They didn't decide to help him.
5. Where was Jessica born?

4

1. True	6. True
2. True	7. True
3. True	8. False
4. False	9. False
5. True	10. False

▶ Page 17

5

1. Why	6. Who
2. Which	7. What
3. When	8. Why
4. Whose	9. Who
5. What	10. Who

6

1. Why didn't you come yesterday?
2. Who wrote the Invisible Man?
3. The Titanic sank in 1912.
4. Did the film begin at 3 o'clock?
5. What did you see when you went to London?

▶ Page 18

GAMES

1. My brother and my sister were born on the same day. My name's Michael.
2. My wife and I had a son and a daughter. My name's Henry.
3. I've got two brothers. My name's Claire.
4. I've got two nephews and one niece. My name's Margaret.
5. My husband and I had only one daughter. My name's Elizabeth.
6. My sister's lucky. She's got two brothers. My name's David.
7. My parents had only one child. My name's Monica.
8. My sister's got one brother. My name's John.
9. My husband and I had one son and one daughter. My name's Victoria.
10. My wife and I have got one child and three grandchildren. My name's Charles.

UNIT 4 WHAT WAS SHE DOING WHEN YOU ARRIVED?

▶ Page 19

1 PISTE 10

It's great to have good friends! I **(1) phoned** some of them last Friday and asked them to come immediately because I **(2) had** a big problem.
The first one I **(3) called** was my old friend Bill. He said he was sorry but he **(4) was having** dinner with his boss at that moment and couldn't come.
Kate was sorry too but she **(5) was going out** with Eddie and it was impossible for her to change her plans.
When I phoned Bruce his wife **(6) told** me he **(7) was painting** the bathroom and she didn't want to disturb him. Peter and Jane **(8) were playing** bridge with friends and said it was impossible to quit. Tony **(9) wasn't doing** anything special but he was very tired and said he preferred staying at home.
Then I phoned my next-door neighbours and they **(10) came** immediately. So I wasn't alone to celebrate my birthday!

2 PISTE 11

1. a. Sam's coming tomorrow night.
2. b. He was waiting for me at the airport.
3. b. She's getting married on Saturday.
4. a. I'm afraid John's taken your computer.
5. c. She's seen her new boss.

▶ Page 20

3 1. Que faisiez-vous lundi dernier entre 10 et 11 heures du matin ?
2. Je crois que je travaillais dans le jardin.
3. Vous êtes sûr ? Il pleuvait fort à ce moment-là.
4. Oh oui je me souviens. Je rangeais mon garage quand Fred Gore a sonné à la grille.
5. Exact. Un voisin l'a vu entrer. Le problème est qu'il n'est jamais réapparu...

4

1. c	*6. a*
2. b	*7. c*
3. a	*8. a*
4. c	*9. c*
5. b	*10. b*

▶ Page 21

5 *1. An elephant is bigger than a hippopotamus.*
2. Tea is as good as coffee.
3. A car is more expensive than a motorbike.
4. My sister is more intelligent than you.
5. A snake is more dangerous than a scorpion.

6 *1. My wife's family is Australian.*
2. Whose shoes are those? / Whose are those shoes?
3. They are Emma's. Clementine's are pink.
4. The Wilsons' two sons live in London.
5. Frank's car is English. Mine is Japanese.

▶ Page 22

7 *1. was dancing*
2. Mine
3. danced
4. yours
5. that
6. than
7. wasn't working
8. Whose
9. Who's
10. didn't work

GAMES

I'm sure you're a great friend...

JE FAIS LE POINT DÉCEMBRE

▶ Page 23

1 PISTE 12
1. He came home last night.
2. What time did you get up last Sunday?
3. They didn't write anything.
4. Didn't you see she was crossing the street?
5. It wasn't raining when I started washing my car.

3 PISTE 13
1. b. When were you born?
2. a. Who wrote Romeo and Juliet?
3. c. Whose children did you see?
4. d. What was he doing when you arrived?
5. c. Did it snow last night?

3 *1. b*
2. b
3. a
4. a
5. b

4 1. Personne n'a trouvé la solution.
2. Ta sœur est pire que toi.
3. A quoi ressemblait-il ?
4. Que s'est-il passé après le dîner ?
5. A qui est ce chapeau ?

5

1. a	*6. a*
2. a	*7. b*
3. b	*8. b*
4. b	*9. b*
5. a	*10. a*

▶ Page 24

6 *1. Julius Caesar invaded Britain in 55 and 54 before Christ.*
2. What happened to Charles Dickens when he was 12?
3. I didn't know that George I wasn't English.
4. Queen Victoria reigned from 1837 to 1901.
5. George Washington became the first president of the USA in 1789.

7
1. Whose car is that?
2. It's mine.
3. I thought it was Claire's.
4. Claire's car is smaller than mine.
5. But it's faster.

8
1. Did he come yesterday?
2. Did they write me a letter?
3. Did Jim understand my question?
4. Did I drink your coffee?
5. Did I go to London in July?

9
1. It rained yesterday.
2. He was working between 5 and 6.
3. The police caught him.
4. They all got killed.
5. The accident happened at night.

UNIT 5 WHAT WILL YOU DO WHEN YOU GROW UP ?

▶ Page 25

1 PISTE 14

Steve: Oh, hello Rebecca! I was looking for you. Are you doing anything special this weekend?
Rebecca: Yes, I am. My sister Jane is arriving tonight from Canada with her husband. He's from Toronto and it's his first time in London.
Steve: Great. What are you going to show them?
Rebecca: I'm going to take them to the Tower of London. Scott teaches history.
Steve: Scott?
Rebecca: Yes, Scott. My sister's husband. You aren't listening, Steve.
Steve: Yes, I am but I was thinking... I'm taking two friends to Stonehenge this Saturday. What about coming with us?
Rebecca: That's a great idea! I'm sure Scott will love it. But...
Steve: What?
Rebecca: There's a problem with my sister. She isn't really fascinated by history...
Steve: ...and you think she'd prefer shopping to Stonehenge...
Rebecca: Shopping? Of course, Steve! That's what we'll do. You go to Stonehenge with Scott and your friends and I'll go shopping with Jane.
Steve: OK but aren't you going to ask Jane and Scott about it?
Rebecca: There won't be any problem Steve. They'll love the idea. I'm going to the airport now. See you Saturday.

1. True	6. True
2. True	7. False
3. False	8. True
4. True	9. False
5. True	10. False

2 PISTE 15
1. I'll have a double cheeseburger and a big coke, please.
2. What are you going to do with that revolver?
3. Hurry up! The film starts at 8 o'clock.
4. Aren't you going to buy a new computer?
5. – Will you marry me one day, Jane?
– No, I won't.

▶ Page 26

3

1. True	6. False
2. False	7. True
3. True	8. True
4. True	9. False
5. False	10. True

4

1. c	6. b
2. a	7. b
3. c	8. a
4. b	9. a
5. a	10. b

▶ Page 27

5

1. any	6. someone
2. some	7. anywhere
3. some	8. something
4. no	9. Nobody
5. anything	10. any

6
1. When will you come and see me?
2. Are you going to buy the most expensive computer in the shop?
3. There's no one left in the house.
4. Jane is the best pupil of her class.
5. I'm leaving tomorrow.

▶ Page 28

GAMES

1. b	6. c
2. a	7. a
3. c	8. a
4. b	9. c
5. c	10. b

UNIT 6 *I'VE BEEN WAITING FOR YOU FOR HOURS!*

▶ Page 29

1 PISTE 16

– At last, here you are, Laura!
– I'm sorry Sean. Have you been waiting long?
– Have I been waiting long? Of course I have! I've been waiting for you for 48 minutes and it's very cold you know.
– I'm sorry, Sean. But you see I met Gordon, we had a drink and we talked...
– You met your ex-boyfriend and you talked! What about me then?
– I know but Gordon was so unhappy...
– Poor Gordon!
– Don't be nasty. You've never liked Gordon.
– Of course I've never liked Gordon. He was your boyfriend.
– Are you jealous?
– Of course I'm jealous!
– Great. Does that mean you really love me?
– Laura. Are you crazy?
– Don't be angry, Sean. I didn't meet Gordon. I just wanted to be sure you loved me and I wasn't late. In fact I waited at that café over there and I watched you waiting...
– Why?
– I said to myself: If he can't even wait for me for half an hour, I'll never see him again. And you waited for 48 minutes! Are you still angry with me?
– No, I'm not. But (he sneezes) I'm really cold now.
– Poor Gor... Poor Sean.
– Laura, that wasn't funny. (She laughs) Let's go and drink something hot.

1. False	6. True
2. False	7. True
3. True	8. False
4. True	9. False
5. True	10. True

2 PISTE 17

1. I've washed your car. It's clean now.
2. Has your brother read Harry Potter and the Goblet of Fire?
3. I've just seen your girlfriend.
4. Chris has been painting for three hours.
5. How long have you been waiting for me?

▶ Page 30

3
1. As-tu fait tes devoirs ?
2. Elle habite à Londres depuis deux semaines.
3. Elle essaie de s'arrêter de fumer depuis Noël.
4. Nous travaillons depuis des heures !
5. Ils ont trouvé le meurtrier.

4

1. a	6. a
2. b	7. a
3. a	8. b
4. b	9. a
5. a	10. a

5
1. A Japanese explorer, Kenji Yuriko, has discovered a temple in Central America.
2. He thinks the Mayas built it seven or eight hundred years ago.
3. When the Spanish arrived, the Mayas abandoned their temple.
4. No one has seen that temple since then.
5. Mr Yuriko has refused to say where the temple is situated to protect it from any "visitors".
3. 5. 1. 4. 2.

▶ Page 31

6
1. How old
2. How tall
3. How far
4. How often
5. How much
6. How long
7. How high
8. How about
9. How many
10. How long

7
1. How many brothers have you got / do you have?
2. How long have you been working?
3. I've understood! It's very simple!
4. When did you understand?
5. She stopped smoking in February.

▶ Page 32

GAMES

How nice to be perfect, isn't it?

JE FAIS LE POINT FÉVRIER

▶ Page 33

1
PISTE 18
1. There will be a big party for my birthday.
2. It's going to snow.
3. Your train leaves at 6.15 am.
4. We're having lunch at Buckingham Palace next Sunday.
5. Will you come? No, I won't.

2
PISTE 19
1. a. Have you understood?
2. b. Won't you come?
3. b. Is it going to rain?
4. a. Have you been waiting long?
5. b. Are they coming next week?

3
1. La baleine est le plus grand mammifère sur terre.
2. La Grande-Bretagne est la huitième île la plus grande du monde.
3. L'Amazone est le second fleuve le plus long du monde.
4. La planète la plus brillante du système solaire est Vénus.
5. Picasso a certainement été le plus prolifique de tous les peintres.

4

1. b	4. a
2. d	5. c
3. e	

5

1. a	6. b
2. a	7. a
3. a	8. b
4. a	9. b
5. a	10. b

▶ Page 34

6

1. nothing	4. somebody
2. any	5. any
3. Some	

7
1. I'm afraid I haven't understood your question.
2. How often did you make your bed last month?
3. He's been swimming for ten minutes.
4. Will you live in the United States when you are married?
5. How long have you known that awful girl?
6. The day I met her was the happiest day in my life.
7. They've been married since 2007.
8. There's something quite strange in this house.
9. No one has ever seen the Loch Ness Monster.
10. Will they ever stop quarrelling?

8

1. How	
2. Who	4. What
3. Where	5. When

UNIT 7 *IF I HAD KNOWN...*

Page 35

1 PISTE 20

– Good morning. I'm Michael Wilson and I had a mail from Mr Walsh yesterday for a job. Can I see Mr Walsh?
– There is no Mr Walsh here.
– No Mr Walsh?
– But there's a Mrs Walsh. That's me. I'm the boss.
– Oh, I'm so sorry, Mrs Walsh.
– It's all right, Mr Wilson. Can I ask you a few questions?
– Yes, of course.
– The job I am offering is two-fold. You'll have to drive my car and accompany me when I meet customers. I buy and sell precious stones.
– That's rather exciting! You need both a chauffeur and a bodyguard.
– Do you think you'll be able to do that?
– Sure. I can drive of course and I practise karate and haikido.
– Exactly what I need. You'll have to work every day from 10am to 5pm.
– No problem.
– And you'll have to accompany me to Europe every two months.
– Wow! That's great! I have never been to Europe.
– OK. You get the job, Mr Wilson.
– Thanks, Mrs Walsh. But please, call me Mike.
– You get the job, Mike. Be here tomorrow morning at 9:30 with your driving licence and get a passport. We're flying to the Netherlands in three weeks.

1. False
2. True
3. True
4. True
5. False
6. True
7. True
8. False
9. False
10. False

2 PISTE 21

1. He said he could play the piano.
2. Will you be able to come tomorrow?
3. Did you have to wait long?
4. They'll have to find another solution.
5. No one was able to open the door.

Page 36

3

1. Il n'avait jamais vu cette jeune fille auparavant.
2. Ils venaient de s'enfuir quand la police est arrivée.
3. Il a dit qu'il avait toujours travaillé le samedi.
4. Il y avait longtemps qu'ils avaient trouvé le trésor.
5. Si seulement il avait été riche !

4 *Jennifer Mackenzie **(1) had** never **(2) been** to Hollywood before. She was from Wyoming where she **(3) lived** and worked on her parents' ranch. Her aunt had **(4) invited** her for a whole month because she needed someone to look after her house.*
*Jennifer's aunt, Peg Baxter, was a voice coach. She **(5) taught** actors and actresses to speak clearly and correctly. And Peg had **(6) gone** to England to coach Betty Benfield, a movie-star more famous for her looks than for the way she acted and **(7) spoke**.*
*One day, Jennifer had a visitor, Bruce Butler. He was very disappointed when Jennifer told him Peg was away. He said he had an audition for a TV series in four days and he had to speak and walk like a cowboy to get the role! Jennifer **(8) knew** nothing about movies but she knew a lot about cowboys. She taught the young man how to walk and talk like a cowboy. He was a good student and four days later he **(9) got** the job!*
*When Peg came back, she laughed when her niece explained what she had done and decided to keep her as an assistant. Jennifer now has a big house in Beverley Hills and is one of the best coaches you can find in California. What about Bruce? He **(10) found** a real job on a ranch in Montana and never came back to Hollywood.*

Page 37

5

1. ø
2. a
3. ø
4. ø
5. the
6. the
7. ø
8. a
9. an
10. ø

6 1. He had never seen the sea.
2. If only I had known you when I was 20!
3. He had finished when I arrived.
4. Time is money.
5. His wife is a dentist.
6. The United States and Canada are neighbours.
7. Do you play the guitar?
8. He'll have to come.
9. I won't be able to help you.
10. Could you do my maths?

▶ Page 38

GAMES

Agatha Christie → Hercule Poirot
Arthur Conan Doyle → Sherlock Holmes
Bob Kane → Batman
Bram Stoker → Count Dracula
Charles Defoe → Robinson Crusoe
Charles Dickens → Oliver Twist
Charles Schulz → Snoopy
Edgar Rice Burroughs → Tarzan
Enyd Blyton → The Famous Five
Ernest Hemingway → The Old Man
George Lucas → Obi-Wan Kenobi
Harriet Beecher Stowe → Uncle Tom
Henry George Wells → The Invisible Man
Ian Fleming → James Bond
James Matthew Barrie → Peter Pan
Joanne Kathleen Rowling → Harry Potter
Johnston McCulley → Zorro
Jonathan Swift → Gulliver
Lewis Carroll → Alice
Margaret Mitchell → Scarlett O'Hara
Mark Twain → Tom Sawyer
Mary Shelley → Frankenstein
Max Groening → Bart Simpson
Roald Dahl → Charlie Bucket
Robert Louis Stevenson → Doctor Jekyll
Rudyard Kipling → Mowgli
Tex Avery → Droopy
Walt Disney → Mickey Mouse
Walter Scott → Ivanhoe
William Shakespeare → Hamlet

UNIT 8 *I'D BUY A COMPUTER IF I COULD...*

▶ Page 39

1 PISTE 22

Bob: *Can I help you?*
Cindy: *Yes. I've never been here before and I'd like to know where the boss's office is.*
Bob: *You mean Mr Turner's office I suppose.*
Cindy: *Yes, that's it. Mr Turner's office. Where is it?*
Bob: *Do you have an appointment, Miss?*
Cindy: *An appointment? Do you mean I have to phone to be allowed to see him?*
Bob: *I'm afraid so, Miss. Mr Turner is a very busy man. Do you want to speak to his secretary?*
Cindy: *Of course I don't. I want to speak to Mr Turner.*
Bob: *I see... Please write your name, your phone number and the object of your visit on this sheet.*
Cindy: *That's ridiculous! Just call him and tell him Cindy wants to see him. It's urgent!*
Bob: *Will you please stop shouting, Miss! You can't see Mr Turner today. That's all!*
(Mr Turner opens door)
Mr Turner: *What's the matter, Bob?*
Bob: *I'm sorry, Mr Turner but this young lady wants to see you and she hasn't got an appointment...*
Cindy: *Dad! Your bodyguard doesn't want me to see you.*
Mr Turner: *Cindy! What are you doing here? Shouldn't you be at school?*
Cindy: *I'm on holiday, Dad. Remember!*
Mr Turner: *Oh, yes, of course. What do you want? Hurry up I'm...*
Cindy: *...very busy, I know. Bob told me.*
Bob: *I'm sorry, Mr Turner. I didn't know you had a daughter.*
Mr Turner: *Not one, Bob. I have four daughters! Now come along, Cindy...*
Cindy: *Bye, Bobby!*
Bob: *Goodbye, Miss Turner.*

1. b
2. b
3. b
4. a
5. b
6. b
7. a
8. a
9. b
10. b

2 PISTE 23

1. What would you do if I gave you $1,000?
2. I'd come if I could.
3. I wouldn't do that if I were you.
4. Would you like to come with me?
5. You could have phoned!

▶ Page 40

3
1. La plupart de ses enfants vivent en Californie.
2. Nous avons eu beaucoup de visiteurs cette semaine.
3. Combien coûte ce T-shirt ?
4. Pourrais-tu me prêter quelques dollars ?
5. Trop de jeunes femmes fument.
6. Je connais très peu de gens à Londres.
7. Il n'y a pas beaucoup de commerces dans mon village.
8. As-tu assez d'argent ?
9. Est-ce que je peux avoir un peu de lait, s'il-te-plaît ?
10. Presque tous mes amis travaillent.

4
1. Forbidden
2. Allowed
3. Forbidden
4. Forbidden
5. Allowed

5
1. a boss
2. an appointment
3. surprised
4. a daughter
5. several

▶ Page 41

6
1. If I could, I'd buy a motorycle.
2. What would you do if you had more money?
3. Wouldn't you like to come?
4. He'd have read the book if he had had time.
5. It might snow.
6. He should try to understand.
7. Shall I open the window?
8. The children weren't allowed to get in.
9. It might rain.
10. You shouldn't laugh.

7
1. Shall
2. 'd
3. allowed
4. enough
5. little

▶ Page 42

GAMES

A	D	R	M	A	N	C	H	E	S	T	E	R	F	B	R	G	H	D	N	J	I	O	T
C	C	A	R	T	H	F	W	A	S	H	I	N	G	T	O	N	V	G	H	J	K	L	T
B	Q	R	T	Y	U	I	I	Y	M	E	L	B	O	U	R	N	E	F	R	T	Y	U	I
C	F	T	H	J	K	N	J	C	D	U	B	L	I	N	A	E	R	C	J	K	I	R	I
E	K	E	G	A	X	F	Z	C	A	N	A	D	A	F	G	R	Y	U	H	K	D	G	D
A	W	Q	W	Z	S	X	E	D	C	I	R	E	L	A	N	D	R	F	V	T	G	B	Y
C	S	H	A	K	E	S	T	E	R	T	O	R	O	N	T	O	V	S	A	E	S	A	R
R	W	H	E	R	E	R	W	A	L	E	S	A	R	E	T	R	H	E	F	L	O	W	E
O	J	O	A	B	B	A	E	S	Y	D	N	E	Y	Z	M	A	T	U	R	B	I	T	R
C	S	L	O	W	H	O	B	O	B	N	E	W	Y	O	R	K	C	I	T	Y	O	T	I
O	S	I	P	E	R	S	A	U	R	A	U	S	T	R	A	L	I	A	P	L	A	T	Y
D	U	S	D	T	H	E	U	N	I	T	E	D	K	I	N	G	D	O	M	E	V	I	L
E	F	Y	A	S	M	J	A	M	A	I	C	A	E	T	A	S	M	A	S	T	U	B	R
K	S	E	X	C	H	I	C	A	G	O	B	T	R	Y	H	J	K	L	O	I	Y	T	E
E	A	U	C	L	A	I	E	D	I	N	B	U	R	G	H	R	D	E	L	A	L	K	U
L	M	O	N	A	D	A	L	L	A	S	M	I	P	I	E	R	S	A	R	K	O	C	H
A	R	A	C	G	I	S	C	A	L	O	S	A	N	G	E	L	E	S	R	D	E	S	T
T	I	N	G	P	O	M	P	J	E	R	S	E	Y	I	D	O	U	M	A	C	M	A	H
Y	N	M	I	T	T	E	R	E	N	G	L	A	N	D	A	N	D	L	A	G	A	R	D
T	M	I	C	A	N	B	E	R	R	A	C	H	E	L	G	O	O	G	Y	E	A	R	D
G	N	L	O	P	C	O	C	L	O	N	D	O	N	V	O	O	L	A	A	L	B	R	U
T	F	O	R	N	O	T	H	I	L	I	V	E	R	P	O	O	L	N	G	J	U	B	E
J	U	N	I	C	O	E	N	E	W	Z	E	A	L	A	N	D	C	H	R	I	S	R	T
K	I	A	N	E	O	T	T	A	W	A	S	Y	U	N	V	R	A	I	N	O	C	J	E
T	H	E	U	N	I	T	E	D	S	T	A	T	E	S	O	F	A	M	E	R	I	C	A
I	A	U	L	R	V	C	A	R	D	I	F	F	O	I	R	A	Q	U	R	L	P	O	I
L	E	S	T	F	R	A	N	S	C	O	T	L	A	N	D	C	H	E	M	E	N	T	C
N	N	C	O	M	R	D	E	S	A	N	F	R	A	N	C	I	S	C	O	I	E	D	S

JE FAIS LE POINT MARS

▶ Page 43

1 PISTE 24

1. It might snow tonight.
2. I'd like to go out next weekend.
3. You should get up at 6 every day.
4. Most of my friends can swim.
5. I'll have to help my sister with her maths.

2 PISTE 25

1. b. A pet which catches mice and birds.
2. a. A piece of furniture you sleep in.
3. b. A room where you get dinner ready.
4. c. Shoes used for games and sports.
5. b. The opposite of a lot.
6. a. The opposite of a few.
7. b. A person who buys something at a store.
8. c. One twelfth of a year.
9. a. You do it when someone asks you a question.
10. b. The day before today.

3

1. would *4. would*
2. had *5. had*
3. would

4

1. Il se pourrait qu'il pleuve cet après-midi.
2. Il ne m'ont pas autorisé à conduire leur voiture.
3. Tu devras te coucher à 10 heures.
4. Je n'avais pas remarqué que tu étais malade.
5. Tu devrais essayer de trouver un meilleur emploi.

▶ Page 44

5

1. a *6. c*
2. c *7. a*
3. c *8. c*
4. b *9. a*
5. a *10. b*

6

1. Everybody had started playing when Jennifer arrived.
2. Did you know he was a private detective?
3. Shall we go home now?
4. Why didn't they allow me to take photos?
5. If I had known, I'd have bought something to drink.

7

1. My sister may come tomorrow.
2. I can say a few words in Chinese.
3. If only I had known!
4. I had never read that poem.
5. Business is business.
6. Breakfast is at 9 o'clock.
7. I don't like tea. I prefer coffee.
8. She's an actress.
9. He'll be able to help you tomorrow.
10. I'll have to invite a few friends next week.

UNIT 9 *HE SAID I WAS THE BEST, DIDN'T HE?*

▶ Page 45

1 PISTE 26

BBC Radio 4. Here is the news.

The Queen has declared she is to meet the French President next month in Paris.
The tallest man in the world is going to get married. His future wife is only 1.83 metres tall.
The cheapest car in the world is Indian. It costs only $2,000.
Green classes are more and more numerous in British schools.
Doctors say children eat too many sweets, drink too much soda and don't eat enough fruit.
More and more people abandon their pets over the Christmas holiday period.
Warren Buffett, is the richest man in the world. Poor Bill Gates is only the third richest man in the world now.
Cheese! Britain has 4.2 million cameras, one for every 14 people in the country.

Each person is caught on camera an average of 300 times daily.
And now the weather. It will rain all day long tomorrow all over Britain. Keep on smiling.

1. False	6. False
2. False	7. False
3. True	8. True
4. True	9. True
5. False	10. False

2 PISTE 27

1. b. How old are you?
2. b. I saw them last night.
3. a. What are you reading?
4. b. I can't drive!
5. a. Tom's downstairs!

▶ Page 46

3

1. a	4. b
2. b	5. b
3. a	

4

1. Last Friday I went to the swimming pool with my friend Dave.
2. On the way we met Dave's ex-girl friend, Kristina Dell.
3. She asked Dave to give her back the letters she had sent him.
4. He said he had burnt them and they both started quarrelling.
5. I left them and went to the swimming pool on my own.

3. 5. 1. 4. 2.

5

1. Qui t'a dit que j'étais le garçon le plus stupide de l'école ?
2. Il m'a dit de ne pas essayer de le rappeler.
3. Elle a dit qu'elle avait essayé de m'envoyer un e-mail.
4. Tom a dit qu'il resterait aussi longtemps que je le souhaitais.
5. Sue a dit qu'après tout il se pourrait qu'elle vienne.

▶ Page 47

6

1. aren't they?	6. mustn't you?
2. don't you?	7. Hasn't he?
3. does she?	8. won't they?
4. didn't it?	9. couldn't he?
5. wouldn't he?	10. wasn't there?

7

1. What's your name?
2. You're stupid!
3. How many brothers do you have? / How many brothers have you got?
4. I don't like you.
5. Can you swim?
6. Yes, I can.
7. Do you play tennis?
8. I invited her last week.
9. I'll help you.
10. We've enjoyed the party!

▶ Page 48

GAMES

Animals	**Clothes**
Elephant	Blazer
Guinea pig	Cap
Monkey	Jeans
Octopus	Raincoat
Oyster	Scarf
Pheasant	Sneakers
Platypus	Socks
Rabbit	Tie
Tortoise	Tights
Vulture	Tracksuit

Food	**House**
Apple-pie	Basement
Beans	Bathroom
Cheese	Cellar
Cherries	Chimney
Chops	Fireplace
Fish' n' chips	Flat
French fries	Floor
Hamburger	Hall
Milkshake	Kitchen
Sausages	Landing

Jobs	**Transport**
Analyst	Cable car
Bodyguard	Car
Coroner	Coach
Engineer	Helicopter
Fisherman	Hovercraft
Lorry-driver	Jet plane
Mechanic	Lorry
Midwife	Moped
Nurse	Scooter
Race-driver	Submarine

UNIT 10 *MADE IN ENGLAND*

▶ Page 49

1 PISTE 28

– Hello, Samantha! Happy birthday to you!
– Thanks, John. That's very nice of you.
– Did you get lots of presents?
– Yes, I did. I was given CDs, books, clothes and money.
– Nothing else?
– Oh, yes. I was also sent a guitar from Barcelona but I don't know anyone there.
– Someone in Barcelona must know you play the guitar I suppose. You've got fans everywhere!
– That's very exciting but I'd like to know who that mysterious fan might be.
– Did you try your guitar?
– Oh, yes I did. I played the guitar at my birthday party and it was a great success.
– It's a pity I couldn't hear that!
– By the way, why didn't you come to my party? A new girlfriend I suppose.
– Not at all. I had to accompany my boss.
– Where to?
– Er... That's a funny coincidence. I went to... Barcelona.
– Oh, John! That was you, then! Thanks a lot, that's a marvellous present. And do you want to know something funny about that guitar?
– Yes, what about it?
– It was made in South Korea.

1. True	*6. False*
2. False	*7. True*
3. True	*8. True*
4. False	*9. False*
5. False	*10. True*

2 PISTE 29

1. The Mona Lisa was painted by Leonardo da Vinci in 1503.
2. America was discovered in 1492 by Christopher Columbus.
3. European astronauts will be sent to Mars before 2050.
4. English is understood everywhere.
5. A new school has been built in my town.

▶ Page 50

3
1. a
2. b
3. a
4. c
5. a
6. c
7. b
8. c
9. a
10. c

4
1. On m'a donné 20 dollars à Noël.
2. On a construit cette maison en 2007.
3. On sert le thé à 5 heures.
4. On réparera demain ma bicyclette.
5. On peut voir un bébé lion au zoo.

5
1. a magazine
2. a mammoth
3. a playwright
4. a mouse
5. Pi

▶ Page 51

6
1. There used to be a garden here.
2. I'm used to working with her.
3. She used to sing all the time.
4. You'll get used to driving a lorry.
5. I used to live in London.

7
1. Bees produce honey.
2. Spielberg directed the film.
3. Eleonor brought this pizza.
4. Ann will write the script.
5. My brother is painting my house.

8
1. Who was Star Wars directed by?
2. There used to be a big park here.
3. Most toys sold in Europe are made in China.
4. You are the only person who likes me!
5. I never understood why she married that ridiculous politician!

▶ Page 52

GAMES

air → heir
aren't → aunt
ate → eight
buy → by
C → see
colonel → kernel
cue → queue
ewe → you
pair → pear
peace → piece
principle → principal
Q → queue
R → are
rap → wrap
serial → cereal
site → sight
flour → flower
for → four
genes → jeans
guessed → guest
hear → here
I → eye
knew → new
knight → night
knows → nose
T → tea
two → too
U → you
war → wore
which → witch
why → Y
won → one
write → right

JE FAIS LE POINT MAI

▶ Page 53

1 PISTE 30
1. He had come, hadn't he?
2. He will come, won't he?
3. He shouldn't come, should he?
4. He came, didn't he?
5. He doesn't have to come, does he?

2 PISTE 31
1. a helicopter
2. a butcher
3. a zoo
4. a flying fish
5. a chimpanzee

3
1. Hier on m'a offert un emploi.
2. On fabrique des voitures bon marché en Inde.
3. On vend la plupart des jouets dans les supermarchés.
4. On produit du thé en Inde.
5. On enverra des hommes sur Mars dans quelques années.

4
1. False
2. True
3. True
4. False
5. True
6. True
7. False
8. True
9. False
10. True

▶ Page 54

5
1. a
2. b
3. c
4. b
5. a

6
1. His proposal was refused.
2. She has been arrested.
3. Bikes are sold in that shop.
4. You will be forgiven.
5. My favourite zebra has been killed.

7
1. Sit down!
2. What's your name.
3. How old are you?
4. Are you married?
5. Yes, I am.
6. How many children do you have? / Have you got?
7. I don't have any.
8. I need a good lorry driver.
9. I can drive any vehicle.
10. You have the job.

8
1. Most of those shirts are made in India.
2. This house was built in 2001.
3. I used to write poems.
4. You didn't work yesterday, did you?
5. He told me he was the best singer in the world.

UNIT 11 *I LOVE CHATTING ON THE NET!*

▶ Page 55

1 PISTE 32

Bruce: *Hi, everybody! Welcome to your favourite TV show Meet your Idol. Tonight we're very lucky because our special guest is the famous pop singer... Britney Lance! (applaudissements)*

Britney: *Good evening, Bruce! Good evening, everybody!*

Bruce: *I'm sure you know our game, Britney...*

Britney: *Of course I do. I watch it as often as I can and I know I'll have to answer two personal questions.*

Bruce: *Great! Meet now one of your greatest fans... Scott Shane.*

Scott Shane: *Good evening, Britney. How happy I am to meet you! I've been your fan ever since you began singing and I have all your CDs.*

Britney: *Wow! How exciting to meet a real fan! What's your job, Scott?*

Scott: *I'm a lorry driver and I listen to you all day long.*

Bruce: *Great! Will you now ask your first question, Scott?*

Scott: *I read you were to go to Hollywood to play an astronaut in a science fiction film. Is that true?*

Britney: *Not at all. No one has ever contacted me in Hollywood. But I'd like to.*

Scott: *What a pity! I'm sure you could be a great actress.*

Britney: *Thanks, Scott. I'll ring you up when I make a film. What's your other question?*

Scott: *Er... Britney...*

Britney: *Yes, Scott.*

Scott: *Will you marry me?*

Britney: *That's a wonderful proposition, Scott, but I'll have to ask my husband first! He's quite jealous you know!*

Scott: *I knew you wouldn't but don't worry. I'll wait!*

1. False	6. False
2. True	7. False
3. True	8. False
4. True	9. True
5. True	10. False

2 PISTE 33

1. *My hobbies are* **painting** *dinosaurs and* **watching** *horror films.*
2. *I have two jobs:* **fixing** *old fridges and* **selling** *them.*
3. *I enjoy* **shopping** *in London and* **buying** *eccentric clothes.*
4. **Protecting** *the gorillas and* **developing** *tourism are Rwanda's chief projects.*
5. **Living** *and* **working** *in a big city is both stressful and exciting.*

▶ Page 56

3

1. a	4. b
2. b	5. b
3. a	

4

1. a	6. b
2. a	7. b
3. b	8. b
4. b / b	9. b
5. a	10. a

5

1. customer	4. passenger
2. patient	5. viewer
3. witness	

▶ Page 57

6

1. How	4. What
2. What	5. What
3. How	

7

1. *Reading is my favourite hobby.*
2. *I hate cooking*
3. *I like doing nothing.*
4. *I began skiing when I was 3 (years old).*
5. *She spends her time surfing the net.*

8

1. *How ridiculous it is to spend your time chatting with your friends!*
2. *He rarely works on Friday afternoons.*
3. *What horrible kids!*
4. *How stupid she seemed to me!*
5. *It's no good trying to find a solution to this mystery.*

▶ Page 58

GAMES

Accept → Approve	*Hate → Detest*
Allow → Permit	*Leave → Depart*
Answer → Solution	*Like Best → Prefer*

Attractive → Charming	*Like → Love*	*Enough → Sufficient*	*Show → Display*
Beat → Strike	*Little → Young*	*Expensive → Costly*	*Shut → Close*
Begin → Start	*Mad → Crazy*	*Extinct → Dead*	*Simple → Easy*
Believe → Think	*Many → Numerous*	*False → Wrong*	*Supporter → Partisan*
Big → Large	*Observe → Perceive*	*Fast → Quick*	*Talk → Chat*
Burst → Explode	*Present → Gift*	*Forbid → Prohibit*	*Tell → Say*
Change → Modify	*Pretty → Beautiful*	*Freedom → Liberty*	*True → Right*
Cry → Weep	*Propose → Suggest*	*Funny → Amusing*	*Unusual → Strange*
Dangerous → Risky	*Rich → Wealthy*	*Great → Excellent*	*Warm → Hot*
Destroy → Ruin	*Scared → Afraid*	*Happen → Take Place*	
Difficult → Hard	*Seat → Chair*	*Happy → Glad*	
Discover → Find	*Seem → Look*		

UNIT 12 *WHAT ABOUT HAVING A BREAK?*

▶ Page 59

1 PISTE 34

Shop-assistant: *Can I help you, Sir?*
Customer: *Yes, Miss. I'd like to buy a computer but I am hesitating. I suppose some are better than others?*
Shop-assistant: *Not exactly. It depends on what you intend to do with it.*
Customer: *I don't know yet but I'd like to surf the internet. Can they all do that?*
Shop-assistant: *Oh, yes, of course. You see when you buy a car, you can buy a Rolls Royce or a Mini Cooper. Both will get you from A to B but for the price of a Rolls Royce you can buy forty mini Coopers.*
Customer: *I see. OK. What I need is a Mini Cooper.*
Shop-assistant: *Desktop or laptop? Are you going to put your computer on your desk or travel with it?*
Customer: *I want it on my desk and I want a big screen.*
Shop-assistant: *Does the price matter?*
Customer: *Of course it does! $1,500 is all I can pay.*
Shop-assistant: *Well. What about this one? It costs $1,299. It has a big 20-inch screen and we sell lots of them.*
Customer: *It looks great. I'll take it.*
Shop-assistant: *I suppose you don't have a printer.*
Customer: *A printer? Is that really necessary?*
Shop-assistant: *Of course it is. But you're lucky. Look! A special offer.You can get it for $1 extra today with your computer.*
Customer: *Do I need anything else?*
Shop-assistant: *You also need a good word processor. Everybody uses that one. It's only $199.*
Customer: *Only $199! This is my lucky day.*
Shop-assistant: *Well. $1,299 for the computer, $1 for the printer and $199 for the word processor. That's $1,499 altogether.*
Customer: *And I still have $1 left for a coffee! Thanks, Miss!*

1. True	*6. False*
2. True	*7. False*
3. False	*8. True*
4. False	*9. True*
5. False	*10. False*

2 PISTE 35

1. a. Open the door, will you?
2. a. What about going out for a change?
3. b. Don't spend all your pocket money buying mangas!
4. b. Go on talking, John!
5. a. Let's have a break!

▶ Page 60

3
1. À qui appartient ce téléphone ?
2. À quelle heure a décollé ton avion ?
3. Il ne ressemble pas du tout à son père.
4. Je veux qu'on me rende mon argent !
5. Il a traversé le lac à la nage en 10 minutes.
6. Quel goût a ta glace ?
7. Il a grimpé à l'arbre et il est tombé.
8. Est-ce que tu penses à moi quand je ne suis pas là ?
9. Elever des enfants n'est pas toujours facile.
10. Tu t'habitueras au sens de l'humour de ton prof de maths.

4
1. a dentist
2. a taxi driver
3. a reporter
4. a mechanic
5. a pilot
6. a shop assistant
7. a surgeon
8. a movie-director
9. a television announcer
10. a banker

▶ Page 61

5
1. What **were the children doing** when the teacher opened the door?
2. **Does he watch** TV every evening?
3. **I'd like** to speak to that boy. He's cute!
4. **I've been working** for five hours. I'm tired!
5. Look! **I've bought** a fantastic racket. I'm going to win the match.
6. **There used to be** pirates in the Caribbean Islands.
7. **I'll marry** you when I'm rich!
8. Corneille **wrote** Le Cid in 1636.
9. Listen! **Someone's crying** upstairs!
10. Jane! What **are you going** to do with that revolver?

6
1. Does Emma look like her mother?
2. How about going to a good restaurant for a change?
3. What subject are you interested in?
4. He said he was disappointed with me.
5. Don't tell me this is the last exercise of the book!

▶ Page 62

GAMES

By the way, didn't you recognize some of your friends?

JE FAIS LE POINT JUIN

▶ Page 63

1
PISTE 36
1. How nice you are!
2. He always spends his holidays in California.
3. What about getting up at 6 tomorrow morning?
4. Surfing the net and chatting with friends are my favourite hobbies.
5. Who does that book belong to?

2
PISTE 37
1. b. What a stupid answer!
2. a. What about helping your mother?
3. b. How old she is!
4. b. I'm sure you'd like to come jogging with me today.
5. b. I don't approve of your going out with that girl.

3
1. a
2. c
3. a
4. c
5. b
6. b
7. b
8. a
9. c
10. b

4
1. jogging
2. shopping
3. cooking
4. swimming
5. modelling

▶ Page 64

5
1. Trouver son chemin dans le métro de Londres n'est pas très facile.
2. Comme ce fut merveilleux de te voir !
3. Il n'avait jamais envisagé de quitter son emploi à Wall Street.
4. Est-ce que tu es sûr que tu vas t'habituer à t'occuper de six rottweilers ?
5. Si seulement il n'avait pas répondu au téléphone ce jour-là !

6
1. How interesting (this is)!
2. He loves playing the violin.
3. What a mistake!
4. She usually gets up at 8.
5. What about going to the zoo?
6. Translate this text into Italian.
7. I had never seen her.
8. What a pity you can't come!
9. She isn't used to working with him.
10. Did it often rain in July?

7
1. will
2. didn't
3. Was
4. 'd / would
5. can't
6. does
7. 's (has)
8. is
9. aren't
10. 'd (had)

DANS LA COLLECTION
100 % DE RÉUSSITE

REMEMBER!

LES *HOW-QUESTIONS*

***How* peut être employé seul :**
– How are you? – I'm fine. Thanks. – Comment vas-tu? – Bien, merci.
Il peut être **suivi d'un adjectif ou d'un adverbe** et permet alors de poser toutes sortes de questions.

How about...?	Que diriez-vous de...?
How much + singulier?	Combien ? Quel est le prix de ?
How many + pluriel?	Combien?
How deep?	Quelle est la profondeur ?
How far?	À quelle distance ?
How high?	Quelle est la hauteur, l'altitude ?
How long?	Quelle est la longueur ?
How often?	Tous les combien ?
How tall?	Quelle est la taille ?
How wide?	Quelle est la largeur ?

How long... sert aussi à **demander depuis quand** dure un fait.
– How long have you been here? – I've been here for three days / since Wednesday.
– Depuis combien de temps es-tu là ? – Je suis là depuis trois jours. / Depuis mercredi.
– How long have you been waiting? – For ten minutes. / Since 1:10.
– Depuis quand attends-tu ? – Depuis 10 minutes. / Depuis 1h10.

MON SCORE | 10

6 Choose the right word.

Choisis le mot ou les mots interrogatifs dans la liste suivante en tenant compte de la réponse proposée.

1. – .... is planet Earth? – It's about 4,54 billion years old.
2. – .... is your sister? – She's 1,78 metres tall!
3. – .... is it from here to London? – About a hundred kilometres.
4. – .... do you go shopping? – Three times a month.
5. – .... is a Rolls Royce? – About $350,000.
6. – .... has she been working? – Two hours.
7. – .... is the Eiffel Tower? – About 300 metres.
8. – .... a drink? – Good idea! I'm thirsty.
9. – .... pages are there in this book? – Sixty-four.
10. – .... is the River Amazon? – 6,500 kilometres.

MON SCORE | 5

7 Translate these sentences.

Traduis ces phrases.

1. Combien de frères as-tu ? ....
2. Depuis combien de temps travailles-tu ? ....
3. J'ai compris ! C'est très simple ! ....
4. Quand as-tu compris ? ....
5. Elle s'est arrêtée de fumer en février. ....

CALCULE TON TAUX DE RÉUSSITE SUR CE CHAPITRE

Entre 100% et 80%, tu as tout compris. BRAVO !
Entre 80% et 60%, c'est bien.
Si tu as moins de 60%, refais les tests dans quelques jours.

	...	/10	1
+	...	/5	2
+	...	/5	3
+	...	/10	4
+	...	/5	5
+	...	/10	6
+	...	/5	7
=	...	/50	

x 2 =

% de réussite

GAMES! DES JEUX !

A quiz. Special boys but girls can read it too!

What sort of boy are you?

1. What would be your favourite means of transport to go to school if you could choose?
a. A motorbike.
b. A horse.
c. A camel.
d. A Ferrari driven by a famous actress.

2. When talking about girls you say they are...
a. Fascinating.
b. Boring.
c. Hard to understand.
d. Unnecessary.

3. What is your favourite sport?
a. Football.
b. Climbing.
c. Karate.
d. Table tennis.

4. What is your favourite activity at the swimming pool?
a. Diving among swimmers.
b. Swimming under water.
c. Splashing everyone around.
d. Watching girls.

5. What is your favourite book?
a. Harry Potter by J.K. Rowling
b. The Murder of Roger Ackroyd by Agatha Christie
c. My maths book.
d. My favourite what?

6. What do you think of adults?
a. They've forgotten they were kids one day.
b. They do what they can.
c. Do they really have to tell me what's best for me?
d. Do you really want me to answer?

You got mostly a's.
You seem really too serious.

You got mostly b's.
You are a typical teenager.

You got mostly C's.
You are a quite normal boy.

You got mostly d's.
You could be worse, but it would be difficult.

JE FAIS LE POINT...

SPÉCIAL BREVET

JE COMPRENDS CE QUE J'ENTENDS

1 J'écoute et je complète ces phrases.

PISTE 18

/5

1. .... a big party for my birthday.
2. ....snow.
3. Your train .... at 6.15 am.
4. ....at Buckingham Palace.................................... .
5. – ....? – No,.................................... .

2 Je trouve la réponse qui convient à chaque question.

PISTE 19

/5

1. a. Yes, I have. / b. Yes, I did.
2. a. No, I don't. / b. No, I won't.
3. a. Yes, it will. / b. Yes, it is.
4. a. No, I haven't. / b. No, he hasn't.
5. a. Yes, they have. / b. No, they aren't.

JE COMPRENDS CE QUE JE LIS

3 Je sais traduire ces phrases.

/5

1. The blue whale is the biggest mammal on Earth.

   ....

2. Great Britain is the eighth largest island in the world.

   ....

3. The Amazon is the second longest river in the world.

   ....

4. The brightest planet of the solar system is Venus.

   ....

5. Picasso was certainly the most prolific of all painters.

   ....

4 Je sais relier logiquement des membres de phrases.

1. I've been living in ■	■ a. going to have for breakfast.
2. I'll visit the Tower of London ■	■ b. London for six years.
3. I have never ■	■ c. she has written.
4. I don't know what I'm ■	■ d. when I go to England.
5. I wonder how many books ■	■ e. been to Manchester.

/5

5 Je sais choisir entre le prétérit et le present perfect.

1. Molière a. died / b. has died on stage in 1673.
2. When I was a kid, I a. have lived / b. lived in Cardiff.
3. When a. did you see / b. have you seen her?
4. – How long a. have you been / b. were you here? – For half an hour.

5. How many lions a. did you kill / b. have you killed when you were in Africa?
6. I a. have met / b. met him three weeks ago.
7. I a. have been cooking / b. was cooking for hours! I'll have break now.
8. Goodbye! I a. spent / b. have spent a wonderful evening with you.
9. I a. knew / b. have known him since he was 20.
10. Look! It a. was raining / b. has been raining.

| 10

JE COMPRENDS ET J'ÉCRIS

6 Je sais compléter ces phrases à l'aide de some, any ou no.

| 5

1. There's .... thing interesting on TV tonight. Let's go out.
2. There are lots of apples on the tree. Do you want ....?
3. .... of these books are very valuable.
4. Look! There's .... body on the island. He's waving to us!
5. There aren't .... children in the park today. It's too cold.

7 Je sais mettre ces mots dans l'ordre.

| 10

1. your / I / I / understood / question / 'm / haven't / afraid / .
....
2. often / did / you / your / how / bed / last / make / month / ?
....
3. ten / he / 's / been / minutes / for / swimming / . ...
4. married / United States / when / will / you / you / are / in / the / live / ?
....
5. long / have / girl / known / awful / how / that / you / ? ....
6. happiest / in / my / day / day / the / I / met / life / was / the / her / .
....
7. married / since / they / 've / 2007 / been / . ...
8. quite / there / 's / in / house / strange / something / this / .
....
9. Loch / no / monster / one / has / seen / ever / the / Ness / .
....
10. quarreling / ever / will / they / stop / ? ....

8 Je sais compléter ces questions par cinq mots interrogatifs différents.

1. – .... often do you play rugby? – Twice a week.
2. – .... are you thinking of? – My boyfriend.
3. – .... are those people from? – Mexico, I suppose.
4. – .... is this chair made of? – Plastic.
5. – .... will she give her answer? – Before Sunday I hope.

| 5

TOTALISE TES POINTS ET MULIPLIE LE TOTAL PAR 2 POUR OBTENIR TON TAUX DE RÉUSSITE

| 50

x 2 =

% de réussite

Entre 100% et 80%, tu as tout compris. BRAVO !
Entre 80% et 60%, c'est bien.
Si tu as moins de 60%, refais les tests dans quelques jours.

▸ LE *PAST PERFECT*
▸ LES ARTICLES *A*, *THE*, *Ø*
▸ *CAN*, *COULD*, *BE ABLE TO*, *MUST* ET *HAVE TO*

unit 7

If I had known...

JE COMPRENDS CE QUE J'ENTENDS

PISTE 20

1 True or false ?

	True	False
1. *This conversation takes place in the afternoon.*		
2. *Michael Wilson is looking for a job.*		
3. *He got an e-mail yesterday offering him a job.*		
4. *His future boss is Mrs Walsh.*		
5. *Mrs Walsh needs a secretary.*		
6. *She sells and buys precious stones.*		
7. *The job Mrs Walsh is offering is two-fold* (= « double »).		
8. *She goes to Africa every two months.*		
9. *Mike doesn't seem to be pleased with the job offer.*		
10. *Mrs Walsh and Mike are flying to the Netherlands tomorrow morning.*		

MON SCORE ...... /10

REMEMBER!

CAN, *COULD*, *BE ABLE TO*, *MUST* ET *HAVE TO*

Can a une seule autre forme, ***could*** qui exprime un passé ou un conditionnel. *I could drive when I was your age.* Je savais conduire à ton âge. *Could you help me?* Pourrais-tu m'aider ?
Be able to remplace *can* au passé ou au futur. *I wasn't able to find a seat on the train.* Je n'ai pas pu trouver de place dans le train. *Will you be able to come?* Pourras-tu venir ?
Must a une seule forme. Il est remplacé par ***have to*** au passé et au futur. *I had to show my passport.* J'ai dû montrer mon passeport. *You won't have to wait.* Tu n'auras pas à attendre.
Remarque : ***Can*** et ***must*** sont des modaux. Ils expriment un point de vue subjectif.
Be able to et ***have to*** expriment un fait objectif. *He can't understand.* Il ne peut pas comprendre. (C'est mon opinion.) *Is he able to do it?* Est-il capable de le faire ? (objectivement).
I must go. Je dois partir. (Je l'ai décidé.) *I have to go.* Je dois partir. (On m'y oblige.)

PISTE 21

2 Listen and complete.

1. *He said he* .... *play the piano.*
2. .... *come tomorrow?*
3. .... *wait long?*
4. .... *find another solution.*
5. .... *open the door.*

MON SCORE ...... /5

JE COMPRENDS CE QUE JE LIS

REMEMBER!

LE *PAST PERFECT*

Il se forme avec l'auxiliaire *had* suivi du participe passé du verbe.
*I **had** never seen that film before.* Je n'avais jamais vu ce film auparavant.
*He **hadn't** left when I arrived.* Il n'était pas parti quand je suis arrivé.
***Had** you ever met that boy?* Avais-tu déjà rencontré ce garçon ?
Le *past perfect* correspond au **plus-que-parfait français**. Il s'emploie
• pour **parler d'un événement antérieur** à un événement passé
*They **had** gone when the fire broke out.* Ils étaient partis quand l'incendie a éclaté.
• pour **passer du discours direct au discours indirect**
I've bought a book. J'ai acheté un livre.
*He said he **had** bought a book.* Il a dit qu'il avait acheté un livre.
• pour **exprimer l'irréel du passé**
***If only** I **had** known...* Si seulement j'avais su...
On emploie fréquemment les adverbes *always, only, never, ever, still, just* avec cette forme verbale.
*I **had never** heard such a silly question!* Je n'avais jamais entendu de question aussi idiote !

MON SCORE | 5

3 Translate these sentences.

1. He had never seen that girl before. ....
2. They had just run away when the police arrived. ....
3. He said he had always worked on Saturdays. ....
4. They had found the treasure a long time ago. ....
5. If only he had been rich! ....

4 Read and complete.

Complète ce texte à l'aide des 10 verbes suivants.
been / found / gone / got / had / invited / knew / lived / spoke / taught

Jennifer Mackenzie 1. .... never 2. .... to Hollywood before. She was from Wyoming where she 3. .... and worked on her parents' ranch. Her aunt had 4. .... her for a whole month because she needed someone to look after her house. Jennifer's aunt, Peg Baxter, was a voice coach: She 5. .... actors and actresses to speak clearly and correctly. And Peg had 6. .... to England to coach Betty Benfield, a movie-star more famous for her looks than for the way she acted and 7. ....

One day, Jennifer had a visitor, Bruce Butler. He was very disappointed when Jennifer told him Peg was away. He said he had an audition for a TV series in four days and he had to speak and walk like a cowboy to get the role! Jennifer 8. .... nothing about movies but she knew a lot about cowboys. She taught the young man how to walk and talk like a cowboy. He was a good student and four days later he 9. .... the job!

When Peg came back, she laughed when her niece explained what she had done and decided to keep her as an assistant. Jennifer now has a big house in Beverley Hills and is one of the best coaches you can find in California. What about Bruce? He 10. .... a real job on a ranch in Montana and never came back to Hollywood.

MON SCORE | 10

JE SAIS M'EXPRIMER

REMEMBER!

LES ARTICLES A, *THE* ET Ø

A **s'emploie devant un son consonne :** *A book, a hat, a uniform.*
An s'emploie **devant un son voyelle :** *an elephant, an hour, an umbrella.*
On emploie *a/an* **pour parler d'une profession.** *He's a programmer.* Il est programmeur.
The vient de *that*. On l'emploie donc **pour un objet précis**. Il a un emploi plus restreint que le, la, les.
I like blue. J'aime le bleu. MAIS *I don't like the blue of his tie.* Je n'aime pas le bleu de sa cravate.
Retiens ces exemples :
the English: les Anglais *the jobless:* les sans-emplois *the homeless:* les SDF
the United States: les États-Unis *the Netherlands:* les Pays-Bas *the earth:* la terre *the sky:* le ciel
the sun: le soleil *the Internet:* Internet
*He plays **the violin**.* Il joue du violon.
ø (ou article zéro, c'est-à-dire : absence d'article). On l'emploie **pour exprimer une généralité**.
I don't like fish. Je n'aime pas le poisson.
Business is business. Les affaires sont les affaires.
Time is money. Le temps c'est de l'argent.
Quelques exemples de noms qui s'emploient sans articles : *breakfast / lunch / dinner / freedom / winter / summer / swimming / dancing / home / time...*
Devant un titre : *The Queen.* Mais devant un nom propre : *Queen Elizabeth.*

5 A, an, the ou ø ?

Choisis l'article qui convient.

MON SCORE /10

1. *Come downstairs! .... breakfast is ready!*
2. *When I grow up, I'll be .... vet!*
3. *Dieticians say .... fruit and vegetables are good for your health.*
4. *Are you interested in .... ecology?*
5. *Red is .... colour I like best.*
6. *Can you tell me .... name of that girl over there?*
7. *.................................. geography is my favourite subject.*
8. *I'll have ....whisky and soda, please.*
9. *That girl has .... exceptional CV. We're going to hire her.*
10. *.................................. Mount Everest is the highest mountain in the world.*

6 Translate these sentences.

1. Il n'avait jamais vu la mer. ....
2. Si seulement je t'avais connu quand j'avais 20 ans ! ....
3. Il avait fini quand je suis arrivé. ....
4. Le temps, c'est de l'argent. ....
5. Sa femme est dentiste. ....
6. Les États-Unis et le Canada sont voisins. ....
7. Est-ce que vous jouez de la guitare ? ....
8. Il devra venir. ....
9. Je ne pourrai pas t'aider. ....
10. Pourrais-tu faire mes maths ? ....

MON SCORE /10

CALCULE TON TAUX DE RÉUSSITE SUR CE CHAPITRE

Entre 100% et 80%, tu as tout compris. BRAVO !
Entre 80% et 60%, c'est bien.
Si tu as moins de 60%, refais les tests dans quelques jours.

	/10	1
+	/5	2
+	/5	3
+	/10	4
+	/10	5
+	/10	6
=	/50	

x 2 =

% de réussite

GAMES! DES JEUX !

Les héros imaginaires ont des créateurs souvent méconnus. Peux-tu joindre chaque personnage de la colonne de gauche à son créateur dans la colonne de droite ? Ces personnages sont des héros de romans, de bandes dessinées, de films ou de feuilletons de télévision. Le premier exemple est fourni.

Agatha Christie •	• Alice
Arthur Conan Doyle •	• Bart Simpson
Bob Kane •	• Batman
Bram Stoker •	• Charlie Bucket
Charles Defoe •	• Count Dracula
Charles Dickens •	• Doctor Jekyll
Charles Schulz •	• Droopy
Edgar Rice Burroughs •	• Frankenstein
Enyd Blyton •	• Gulliver
Ernest Hemingway •	• Hamlet
George Lucas •	• Harry Potter
Harriet Beecher Stowe •	• Hercule Poirot
Henry George Wells •	• Ivanhoe
Ian Fleming •	• James Bond
James Matthew Barrie •	• Mickey Mouse
Joanne Kathleen Rowling •	• Mowgli
Johnston McCulley •	• Obi-Wan Kenobi
Jonathan Swift •	• Oliver Twist
Lewis Carroll •	• Peter Pan
Margaret Mitchell •	• Robinson Crusoe
Mark Twain •	• Scarlet O'Hara
Mary Shelley •	• Sherlock Holmes
Max Groening •	• Snoopy
Roald Dahl •	• Tarzan
Robert Louis Stevenson •	• The famous Five
Rudyard Kipling •	• the Invisible Man
Tex Avery •	• The Old Man
Walt Disney •	• Tom Sawyer
Walter Scott •	• Uncle Tom
William Shakespeare •	• Zorro

▸ L'EXPRESSION DU CONDITIONNEL
▸ LES QUANTIFIEURS
▸ *MAY, MIGHT, BE ALLOWED TO* ET *SHALL, SHOULD*

unit 8

I'd buy a computer if I could

JE COMPRENDS CE QUE J'ENTENDS

PISTE 22

1 a or b?

Choisis la bonne solution.

1. Bob a. is the boss. / b. works at the reception desk.
2. Cindy a. knows / b. doesn't know Bob.
3. Cindy a. phoned / b. didn't phone before coming.
4. Mr Turner is a. a businessman / b. a secretary.
5. Cindy a. has an appointment with / b. just wants to see Mr Turner.
6. Cindy a. goes away / b. gets angry when Bob tells her she can't see Mr Turner.
7. Mr Turner a. hears / b. doesn't hear Cindy shout.
8. Mr Turner a. is / b. isn't surprised to see his daughter.
9. Cindy has a. no sisters. / b. several sisters.
10. Bob is a. amused / b. embarrassed when he understands Cindy is his boss's daughter.

MON SCORE | 10

REMEMBER!

L'EXPRESSION DU CONDITIONNEL

On utililise l'auxiliaire modal ***would* suivi d'une base verbale**, pour exprimer un conditionnel.
Would se contracte en ***'d*** et en ***wouldn't*** à la forme négative.
*If I **had** more money, I**'d** buy a computer.* Si j'avais plus d'argent, j'achèterais un ordinateur.
*I **wouldn't** like to be your teacher!* Je n'aimerais pas être ton professeur !
Comme en français, on parle de conditionnel de politesse :
*I**'d** like to ask you a question.* J'aimerais te poser une question.
Remarque : *Would* peut être employé avec une base verbale au présent ou au passé (*have* + participe passé) : *He **would like** to come to your party.* Il aimerait venir à ta fête.
*He **would have liked** to come to your party.* Il aurait aimé venir à ta fête.
Le conditionnel est aussi rendu par l'emploi des modaux ***could, might, should***...
***Could** you help me?* Pourriez-vous m'aider ? *He **might** be late.* Il se pourrait qu'il soit en retard.

PISTE 23

2 Listen and complete.

1. What .... you do if I .... you $1,000?
2. I'.................................. come if I ....
3. I .... do that if I .... you.
4. .... you like to come with me?
5. You .... have ....!

MON SCORE | 5

JE COMPRENDS CE QUE JE LIS

REMEMBER!

LES QUANTIFIEURS

Ils indiquent le nombre (*a few children :* quelques enfants) **ou la quantité** (*a lot of work :* beaucoup de travail).
Retiens les principaux quantifieurs. Ils répondent aux questions en :
How much + singulier ? Combien, quel est le prix, quelle quantité... ?
How many + pluriel ? Combien, quel nombre... ?

Devant les dénombrables au pluriel	Devant les indénombrables au singulier
no *friends and* ***no*** *money* pas d'amis et pas d'argent	
(very) ***few*** *friends :* (très) peu d'amis	*(very)* ***little*** *money :* (très) peu d'argent
a few *friends :* quelques amis	***a little*** *money :* un peu d'argent
enough *money and friends :* assez d'amis et assez d'argent	
many / a lot of *friends :* beaucoup d'amis	***much / a lot of*** *money :* beaucoup d'argent
lots of / plenty of *friends and money :* des quantités / plein d'amis et d'argent	
too many *friends :* trop d'amis	***too much*** *money :* trop d'argent
most of *my friends :* la plupart de mes amis	***most of*** *my money :* la plus grande partie de mon argent
all *my friends :* tous mes amis	***all*** *my money :* tout mon argent

3 Translate.

MON SCORE ... /10

1. *Most of her children live in California.* ....
2. *We've had a lot of visitors this week.* ....
3. *How much is that T-shirt?* ....
4. *Could you lend me a few dollars?* ....
5. *Too many young women smoke.* ....
6. *I know very few people in London.* ....
7. *There aren't many shops in my village.* ....
8. *Do you have enough money?* ....
9. *Can I have a little milk, please?* ....
10. *Nearly all my friends work.* ....

4 Allowed or forbidden?

MON SCORE ... /5

Est-ce autorisé ou interdit en Angleterre?	*Allowed*	*Forbidden*
1. *Smoking in public buildings in England.*		
2. *Walking and sitting on the grass in parks.*		
3. *Talking to bus drivers when the bus is moving.*		
4. *Bringing your dog to the swimming pool.*		
5. *Using mobile phones in the streets.*		

5 Find the word.

Trouve les cinq mots définis ci-dessous, qui apparaissent tous dans l'exercice 1 page 39.

1. *A person who hires workers and gives them a salary.* ....
2. *A meeting with someone at a certain place and time.* ....
3. *What you feel when something happens suddenly or unexpectedly.* ....
4. *A female child.* ....
5. *The opposite of "a few"* ....

MON SCORE ... /5

JE SAIS M'EXPRIMER

REMEMBER!

MAY, MIGHT, BE ALLOWED TO ET SHALL, SHOULD

May et ***might*** peuvent exprimer une possibilité.
*We **may** win the match.* Il se peut qu'on gagne le match.
*We **might** win the match.* Il se pourrait qu'on gagne. (plus incertain)
May peut exprimer la permission, mais il est remplacé au passé et au futur par ***be allowed to*** (être autorisé à).
***Were** you **allowed to** take photos?* Est-ce que l'on t'a autorisé à prendre des photos ?
*You **won't be allowed to** get in.* On ne te laissera pas entrer.
Shall sert à proposer un service ou à faire une suggestion.
***Shall** I carry your bag?* Voulez-vous que je porte votre sac ?
***Shall** we have a drink?* Que diriez-vous de boire quelque chose ?
Should sert à exprimer un conseil plus ou moins accentué ou à reprocher quelque chose.
*You **should** stop smoking.* Tu devrais t'arrêter de fumer.
***Shouldn't** you drive more carefully?* Est-ce que tu ne devrais pas conduire plus lentement ?
*You **should** have come.* Tu aurais dû venir.

MON SCORE | 10

6 Translate.

1. Si je pouvais, j'achèterais une moto. ....
2. Que ferais-tu si tu avais plus d'argent ? ....
3. N'aimerais-tu pas venir ? ....
4. Il aurait lu le livre s'il avait eu le temps. ....
5. Il se pourrait qu'il neige. ....
6. Il devrait essayer de comprendre. ....
7. Veux-tu que j'ouvre la fenêtre ? ....
8. Les enfants n'étaient pas autorisés à entrer. ....
9. Il se pourrait qu'il pleuve. ....
10. Tu ne devrais pas rire. ....

7 Complete these sentences.

MON SCORE | 5

Ajoute un seul mot par phrase.

1. .... *we go dancing tonight?*
2. *Oh, yes, I'* .... *like to!*
3. *Are you sure we'll be* .... *to get into the club?*
4. *Yes, I do. But I'm not sure I'll have* .... *money to buy you a drink!*
5. *No problem. I'll ask Mum to give me a* .... *money.*

CALCULE TON TAUX DE RÉUSSITE SUR CE CHAPITRE

Entre 100% et 80%, tu as tout compris. BRAVO !
Entre 80% et 60%, c'est bien.
Si tu as moins de 60%, refais les tests dans quelques jours.

| 10 [1] + | 10 [6] |
+ | 5 [2] + | 5 [7] |
+ | 10 [3]
+ | 5 [4]
+ | 5 [5] = | 50

x 2 = % de réussite

GAMES!

DES JEUX !

Découvre dans cettre grille 25 pays et villes anglophones. Elle se lit de gauche à droite. Raie les lettres inutiles comme il est montré dans la première ligne. Les noms en plusieurs parties sont écrits sans espace. Une des lignes verticales désigne une célèbre organisation internationale.

~~A~~	~~D~~	~~R~~	M	A	N	C	H	E	S	T	E	R	~~F~~	~~B~~	~~R~~	~~G~~	~~H~~	~~D~~	~~N~~	~~J~~	~~I~~	~~O~~	~~T~~
C	C	A	R	T	H	F	W	A	S	H	I	N	G	T	O	N	V	G	H	J	K	L	T
B	Q	R	T	Y	U	I	I	Y	M	E	L	B	O	U	R	N	E	F	R	T	Y	U	I
C	F	T	H	J	K	N	J	C	D	U	B	L	I	N	A	E	R	C	J	K	I	R	I
E	K	E	G	A	X	F	Z	C	A	N	A	D	A	F	G	R	Y	U	H	K	D	G	D
A	W	Q	W	Z	S	X	E	D	C	I	R	E	L	A	N	D	R	F	V	T	G	B	Y
C	S	H	A	K	E	S	T	E	R	T	O	R	O	N	T	O	V	S	A	E	S	A	R
R	W	H	E	R	E	R	W	A	L	E	S	A	R	E	T	R	H	E	F	L	O	W	E
O	J	O	A	B	B	A	E	S	Y	D	N	E	Y	Z	M	A	T	U	R	B	I	T	R
C	S	L	O	W	H	O	B	O	B	N	E	W	Y	O	R	K	C	I	T	Y	O	T	I
O	S	I	P	E	R	S	A	U	R	A	U	S	T	R	A	L	I	A	P	L	A	T	Y
D	U	S	D	T	H	E	U	N	I	T	E	D	K	I	N	G	D	O	M	E	V	I	L
E	F	Y	A	S	M	J	A	M	A	I	C	A	E	T	A	S	M	A	S	T	U	B	R
K	S	E	X	C	H	I	C	A	G	O	B	T	R	Y	H	J	K	L	O	I	Y	T	E
E	A	U	C	L	A	I	E	D	I	N	B	U	R	G	H	R	D	E	L	A	L	K	U
L	M	O	N	A	D	A	L	L	A	S	M	I	P	I	E	R	S	A	R	K	O	C	H
A	R	A	C	G	I	S	C	A	L	O	S	A	N	G	E	L	E	S	R	D	E	S	T
T	I	N	G	P	O	M	P	J	E	R	S	E	Y	I	D	O	U	M	A	C	M	A	H
Y	N	M	I	T	T	E	R	E	N	G	L	A	N	D	A	N	D	L	A	G	A	R	D
T	M	I	C	A	N	B	E	R	R	A	C	H	E	L	G	O	O	G	Y	E	A	R	D
G	N	L	O	P	C	O	C	L	O	N	D	O	N	V	O	O	L	A	A	L	B	R	U
T	F	O	R	N	O	T	H	I	L	I	V	E	R	P	O	O	L	N	G	J	U	B	E
J	U	N	I	C	O	E	N	E	W	Z	E	A	L	A	N	D	C	H	R	I	S	R	T
K	I	A	N	E	O	T	T	A	W	A	S	Y	U	N	V	R	A	I	N	O	C	J	E
T	H	E	U	N	I	T	E	D	S	T	A	T	E	S	O	F	A	M	E	R	I	C	A
I	A	U	L	R	V	C	A	R	D	I	F	F	O	I	R	A	Q	U	R	L	P	O	I
L	E	S	T	F	R	A	N	S	C	O	T	L	A	N	D	C	H	E	M	E	N	T	C
N	N	C	O	M	R	D	E	S	A	N	F	R	A	N	C	I	S	C	O	I	E	D	S

JE FAIS LE POINT...

JE COMPRENDS CE QUE J'ENTENDS

1 J'écoute et je copie ce que l'on me dicte. (PISTE 24) … / 5

1. ....
2. ....
3. ....
4. ....
5. ....

2 Je comprends de quoi l'on parle. (PISTE 25) … / 10

1. a. a goldfish / b. a cat / c. a dog
2. a. a bed / b. a table / c. a bike
3. a. a bathroom / b. a kitchen / c. a garage
4. a. twisters / b. scissors / c. sneakers
5. a. much / b. a little / c. enough
6. a. many / c. enough / d. fewer
7. a. a character / b. a customer / c. a challenger
8. a. a moth / b. a mouth / c. a month
9. a. answer / b. advise / c. agree
10. a. tomorrow / b. yesterday / c. Monday

JE COMPRENDS CE QUE JE LIS

… / 5

3 Je sais distinguer la valeur de 'd selon qu'il correspond à had ou would.

	Had	Would
1. He'd like to come to your party.		
2. They'd forgotten to write to him.		
3. I'd have liked to be a great musician.		
4. She said she'd read my book if she could.		
5. He'd already put on his skis when I arrived.		

4 Je sais traduire ces phrases.

1. It might rain this afternoon. ....
2. They didn't allow me to drive their car. ....
3. You'll have to go to bed at 10. ....
4. I hadn't noticed you were ill. .... … / 5
5. You should try find a better job. ....

5 Je comprends et je choisis le mot qui convient dans chaque phrase.

1. a. If / b. When / c. As I could, I'd buy a new house.
2. Her sister is a. the / b. ø / c. a pop singer.
3. Help! I a. mustn't / b. shouldn't / c. can't swim! | 10
4. They sky is grey! It a. shall / b. may / c. has to rain soon.
5. There's a. too much / b. too many / c. enough sugar in this coffee. I won't drink it.
6. a. A / b. The / c. ø schoolchildren wear uniforms in England.
7. They a. will / b. would / c. have come when their car has been repaired.
8. He a. had / b. has / c. ø forgot to come yesterday.
9. He told me that he a. had / b. has / c. ø found fossils in his garden.
10. The opposite of a little is a. a few / b. a lot / c. several.

JE COMPRENDS ET J'ÉCRIS

6 Je mets ces mots dans l'ordre.

| 5

1. Jennifer / everybody / started / had / arrived / when / playing / .
....
2. a / he / private / you / was / know / did / detective / ?
....
3. we / shall / home / now / go / ? ....
4. didn't / why / allow / to / photos / me / they / take / ?
....
5. I / I / if / have / had / 'd / known / bought / drink / something / to / .
....

7 Je sais traduire ces phrases.

1. Il se peut que ma sœur vienne demain. ....
2. Je sais dire quelques mots en chinois. ....
3. Si seulement j'avais su ! ....
4. Je n'avais jamais lu ce poème. ....
5. Les affaires sont les affaires. .... | 10
6. Le petit déjeuner est à 9 heures. ....
7. Je n'aime pas le thé. Je préfère le café. ....
8. Elle est actrice. ....
9. Il pourra vous aider demain. ....
10. Il me faudra inviter quelques amis la semaine prochaine.
....

TOTALISE TES POINTS ET MULIPLIE LE TOTAL PAR 2 POUR OBTENIR TON TAUX DE RÉUSSITE

| 50

x 2 =

% de réussite

Entre 100% et 80%, tu as tout compris. BRAVO !
Entre 80% et 60%, c'est bien.
Si tu as moins de 60%, refais les tests dans quelques jours.

LE DISCOURS INDIRECT
COMMENT TRADUIRE « QUE » ?
LES *TAGS* INTERROGATIFS

He said I was the best, didn't he?

9 unit

JE COMPRENDS CE QUE J'ENTENDS

PISTE 26

1 True or false?

Ces dix affirmations portent sur les informations télévisées.

	True	False
1. The Queen and the French President are going to meet in London.		
2. The tallest woman in the world is getting married.		
3. You can buy an Indian car for $2,000.		
4. English children are interested in ecology.		
5. Children should eat more sweets and less fruit.		
6. It's a good idea to give someone a pet as a Christmas present.		
7. Bill Gates has serious money problems.		
8. You say Cheese! to people when you want them to smile.		
9. The English are caught on camera about 300 times every day.		
10. The weather will be sunny tomorrow in England.		

MON SCORE | 10

REMEMBER!

LE DISCOURS INDIRECT

Le discours indirect permet de **rapporter ce que quelqu'un a dit**.
« Reste avec moi ! » → Il m'a dit de rester avec lui. *"Stay with me!" → He told me to stay with him.*
Attention aux changements de temps et de personnes :
He said : "I'm late." → He said he was late.
She asked: "Can I help you?" She asked if she could help me.
Le discours indirect est employé avec les verbes ***say, tell, ask, answer, declare***...
She told me: "I'll never marry you." She told me (that) she would never marry me.

PISTE 27

2 a or b?

MON SCORE | 5

Choisis la phrase qui rapporte le mieux chacune des phrases prononcées.

1. a. He asked me how I was. / b. He asked me how old I was.
2. a. She said that I had seen them last night. / b. She said that she had seen them last night.
3. a. He asked me what I was reading. / b. He asked me if I was reading.
4. a. She said she could drive. / b. She said she couldn't drive.
5. a. He told me Tom was downstairs. / b. He told me to come downstairs.

REMEMBER!

COMMENT TRADUIRE « QUE » ?

Que se traduit par
- ***what*** dans une question

What do you want to buy? Que veux-tu acheter ?
- ***than*** ou ***as*** dans une comparaison

Tea is better ***than*** *coffee.* Le thé est meilleur que le café.
Jane is as tall ***as*** *Tarzan.* Jane est aussi grande que Tarzan.
- ***that*** ou **ø** après *say* ou *tell*

He told me ***(that)*** *he was exhausted.* Il m'a dit qu'il était épuisé.
- ***that***, **ø** ou ***what*** quand il est pronom relatif

The book ***(that)*** *I bought cost £9.* Le livre que j'ai acheté coûtait 9 livres.
Tell me ***what*** *you prefer.* Dis moi ce que tu préfères.
- ***une proposition infinitive*** dans des expressions telles que « vouloir que », « J'aimerais que... »

She wanted me ***to help*** *her.* Elle voulait que je l'aide.

3 a or b?

Choisis la bonne réponse.

MON SCORE | 5

1. Jupiter is bigger a. than / b. that Saturn.
2. I'd like a. that you come / b. you to come to my birthday-party.
3. The man a. ø / b. than I'll marry will be handsome, rich and intelligent.
4. Why didn't she say a. what / b. that she wasn't able to repair my computer?
5. Is she as serious a. than / b. as she pretends to be?

4 The right order.

Mets ces phrases dans le bon ordre.

1. She asked Dave to give her back the letters she had sent him.
2. I left them and went to the swimming pool on my own.
3. Last Friday I went to the swimming pool with my friend Dave.
4. He said he had burnt them and they both started quarrelling.
5. On the way we met Dave's ex-girl friend, Kristina Dell.

MON SCORE | 5

5 Translate these sentences.

1. Who told you I was the most stupid boy in the school? ....
2. He told me not to try to call him again. ....
3. She said she'd tried to send me an e-mail. ....
4. Tom said he'd stay as long as I wished. ....
5. Sue said she might come after all. ....

MON SCORE | 5

REMEMBER!

LES *TAGS*

Après avoir déclaré quelque chose, **on confirme ce que l'on a dit à l'aide d'un *tag***, sorte de mini-question en fin d'énoncé.
Ce *tag* est inversé par rapport à la déclaration principale.
*You**'re** French, **aren't you**?* Tu es français, n'est-ce pas ?
*You **aren't** French, **are you**?* Tu n'es pas français, n'est-ce pas ?
On utilise le même auxiliaire que dans la déclaration.
*He**'ll** come next week, **won't he**?* Il viendra la semaine prochaine, n'est-ce pas ?
S'il n'y a pas d'auxiliaire, on utilise *do / did*.
*He **bought** a car, **didn't he**?* Il a acheté une voiture, n'est-ce pas ?
Avec *there is / there are* on reprend la même locution.
*There **is** no answer, **is there**?* Il n'y a pas de réponse, n'est-ce pas ?
Les composés de *some*, *any* et *no* sont repris par *they*.
*Everyone **liked** the film, **didn't they**?* Tout le monde a aimé le film, n'est-ce pas ?

6 Complete these sentences.

Complète chaque phrase par un *tag*.

1. *Kangaroos are mammals,* ....?
2. *You have lunch at school,* ....?
3. *You sister doesn't play rubgy,* ....?
4. *It rained last night,* ....?
5. *He'd buy a car if he could,* ....?
6. *You must go now,* ....?
7. *He's understood the question,* ....?
8. *Everybody will come to my party,* ....?
9. *The president could change his mind,* ....?
10. *There was an accident,* ....?

MON SCORE | 10

7 What did he/she say?

Passe du discours indirect au discours direct comme dans le premier exemple.

1. *He asked me what my name was.* → *"What's your name?"*
2. *He told me I was stupid.* ....
3. *He asked me how many brothers I had.* ....
4. *She told me she didn't like me.* ....
5. *He asked me if I could swim.* ....
6. *I answered I could.* ....
7. *He asked my if I played tennis.* ....
8. *He told me he had invited her the week before.* ....
9. *She told me she would help me.* ....
10. *They said they had enjoyed the party.* ....

MON SCORE | 10

CALCULE TON TAUX DE RÉUSSITE SUR CE CHAPITRE

Entre 100% et 80%, tu as tout compris. BRAVO !
Entre 80% et 60%, c'est bien.
Si tu as moins de 60%, refais les tests dans quelques jours.

	___ / 10	1
+	___ / 5	2
+	___ / 5	3
+	___ / 5	4
+	___ / 5	5
+	___ / 10	6
+	___ / 10	7
=	___ / 50	
x 2 =	___ % de réussite	

GAMES!
DES JEUX !

Place ces 60 mots, présentés ici par ordre alphabétique, dans le groupe qui leur correspond. Il y a 10 mots par catégorie.

Analyst
Apple-pie
Basement
Bathroom
Beans
Blazer
Bodyguard
Cable Car
Cap
Car
Cellar
Cheese
Cherries
Chimney
Chops
Coach
Coroner
Elephant
Engineer
Fireplace
Fish' n' Chips
Fisherman
Flat
Floor
French Fries
Guinea Pig
Hall
Hamburger
Helicopter
Hovercraft
Jeans
Jet Plane
Kitchen
Landing
Lorry
Lorry-driver
Mechanic
Midwife
Milkshake
Monkey
Moped
Nurse
Octopus
Oyster
Pheasant
Platypus
Rabbit
Race-driver
Raincoat
Sausages
Scarf
Scooter
Sneakers
Socks
Submarine
Tie
Tights
Tortoise
Tracksuit
Vulture

Animals	Clothes	Food	Jobs	House	Transport

- **LA VOIX PASSIVE**
- **LES RELATIFS**
- ***USED TO* ET *BE/GET USED TO***

Made in England

unit 10

JE COMPRENDS CE QUE J'ENTENDS

PISTE 28

1 True or false?

	True	False
1. John is calling Samantha to wish her a happy birthday.		
2. Samantha got few birthday presents.		
3. She got a present from a mysterious stranger.		
4. That present was a guitar sent from Italy.		
5. Samantha wasn't pleased to receive that present.		
6. Samantha can't play the guitar.		
7. John couldn't come to Samantha's birthday party.		
8. Samantha thinks he preferred to go out with his girlfriend.		
9. John went to Barcelona with his new girlfriend.		
10. The mysterious present was sent by John.		

MON SCORE |10

REMEMBER!

LA VOIX PASSIVE

On la forme avec l'auxiliaire *BE* suivi du participe passé du verbe. Le complément d'agent, lorsqu'il y en a un, est introduit par *by*. *Hamlet* ***was written by*** *Shakespeare.* *Hamlet* a été écrit par Shakespeare.
L'élément qui agit (l'agent) souvent n'est pas nommé
- parce qu'il n'est pas connu : *My car* ***was stolen*** *yesterday.* Ma voiture a été volée hier.
- parce que c'est évident ou sans intérêt : *Most video cameras* ***are made*** *in Japan.*
La plupart des camescopes sont fabriqués au Japon.
Cette forme est plus employée qu'en français où l'on utilise souvent une forme active ayant pour sujet ON : *I was given $50 for my birthday.* On m'a donné 50 dollars pour mon anniversaire.

PISTE 29

2 Listen and complete.

Écoute et choisis ce que veut dire le locuteur.

MON SCORE |5

1. The Mona Lisa .... *Leonardo da Vinci in 1503.*
2. America .... *by Christopher Columbus.*
3. European astronauts .... *to Mars before 2050.*
4. English .... *everywhere.*
5. A new school .... *in my town.*

REMEMBER!

LES RELATIFS

Who, which, that, whose

Who est le pronom relatif sujet pour les humains.
The boy who is singing is my brother. Le garçon qui chante est mon frère.
That est le pronom complément pour les humains et non-humains (il est souvent omis).
The girl (that) you met was my sister. La fille que tu as rencontrée est ma sœur.
The phone (that) you've bought is fantastic! Le téléphone que tu as acheté est extraordinaire !
Which est le pronom relatif sujet ET complément pour les non-humains. Il peut parfois être remplacé par **that**. *The computer which is in my office is Japanese.* L'ordinateur qui est dans mon bureau est japonais.
The car which/that you repaired was mine. La voiture que tu as réparée était à moi.
Whose s'applique à une relation de possession. (Cette tournure est peu fréquente.) *The person whose car was stolen was my mother.* La personne dont on a volé la voiture, c'était ma mère.

What, which

What annonce ce qui vient et *which* reprend ce qui a été dit. *Tell me what you're going to do.* Dis-moi ce que tu vas faire. *He hit me, which was a mistake.* Il m'a frappé, ce qui fut une erreur.
Attention : « Tout ce que » se traduit par *all that* (et non pas ~~*all what*~~).

Where, when, why Ils ont un antécédent en général implicite, c'est-à-dire non précisé.
I don't know (the place) where and (the day) when he was born. Je ne sais pas où et quand il est né.
Tell me (the reason) why you didn't come yesterday. Dis-moi pourquoi tu n'es pas venu hier.

3 a, b or c?

MON SCORE | 10

Choisis le relatif qui convient. ø signifie que le relatif est sous-entendu.

1. The first man a. who / b. Ø / c. which walked on the moon was Neil Armstrong.
2. The book a. who / b. Ø / c. where I lost was my maths teacher's.
3. Are you the girl a. whose / b. who / c. what boyfriend has just been arrested?
4. Do you know a. when / b. what / c. where he comes from?
5. She smokes a lot, a. which / b. Ø / c. what is bad for her health.
6. She was the only person a. what / b. which / c. that could understand me.
7. He never told us a. what / b. why / c. whose he left his country.
8. Most of the dinosaurs a. who / b. what / c. which lived there were very small.
9. Tarzan never forgot the day a. when / b. which / c. where he met Jane for the first time.
10. Is that all a. what / b. which / c. Ø you can tell me about Clementine?

4 Translate.

MON SCORE | 5

Traduis ces phrases par une phrase ayant pour sujet ON.

1. I was given $20 at Christmas. ....
2. That house was built in 2007. ....
3. Tea is served at 5 o'clock. ....
4. My bike will be repaired tomorrow. ....
5. A baby lion can be seen at the zoo. ....

5 Find the word.

Lis ces cinq définitions et trouve la solution dans cette liste de 10 noms. Seuls cinq noms correspondent aux définitions.

elephant / magazine / mammoth / mouse / newspaper / novelist / pi / pie / playwright / rat

1. A weekly publication with stories, articles, and illustrations in it. ....

2. A large kind of elephant that lived during the Pleistocene and disappeared about 10,000 years ago. ....

3. A writer who is specialized in dramas, tragedies or comedies. ....

4. The part of a computer which was given the name of an animal. ....

5. The ratio of the circumference of a circle to its diameter, roughly equal to 3,14 and usually written with a Greek letter ....

MON SCORE | 5

JE SAIS M'EXPRIMER

REMEMBER!

USED TO ET BE/GET USED TO

Used to est employé pour parler de ce qui était et qui n'est plus ou de ce qui se faisait et ne se fait plus.
*There **used to** be a school here.* Avant il y avait une école ici. *I **used to** play tennis.* Avant je jouais au tennis.
Distingue bien ces trois constructions
*He **used to** get up early.* Autrefois il se levait tôt.
*He **is** used to getting up early.* Il est habitué à se lever tôt. (= ***be*** *used to* + ***V-ing***)
*He'll **get** used to getting up early.* Il s'habituera à se lever tôt. (= ***get*** *used to* + ***V-ing***)

MON SCORE | 5

6 Translate.

Complète ces traductions.

1. Dans le temps, il y avait un jardin ici. *There used* ....
2. J'ai l'habitude de travailler avec elle. *I'm used to* ....
3. Elle chantait tout le temps. *She used to* ....
4. Tu t'habitueras à conduire un camion *(lorry)*.
You'll get used to ....
5. Avant, j'habitais à Londres. *I used to* ....

7 Transform the sentences.

Passe de la forme passive à la forme active.

MON SCORE | 5

1. *Honey is produced by bees.* ....
2. *The film was directed by Spielberg.* ....
3. *This pizza has been brought by Eleonor.* ....
4. *The script will be written by Ann.* ....
5. *My house is being painted by my brother.* ....

8 Make sentences.

1. *was / who / Star Wars / by / directed / ?* .... ?
2. *here / be / a / used / to / big / there / park / .* ....
3. *toys / are / in / in / China / most / Europe / sold / made / .*
....
4. *You/ the / are / only / that / person / me / likes / .* ....
5. *politician / I / understood / why / she / that / married / never / ridiculous / !*
.... !

MON SCORE | 5

CALCULE TON TAUX DE RÉUSSITE SUR CE CHAPITRE

Entre 100% et 80%, tu as tout compris. BRAVO !
Entre 80% et 60%, c'est bien.
Si tu as moins de 60%, refais les tests dans quelques jours.

	| 10	1
+	| 5	2
+	| 10	3
+	| 5	4
+	| 5	5
+	| 5	6
+	| 5	7
+	| 5	8
=	| 50	

x 2 =

% de réussite

GAMES! DES JEUX !

Des homophones sont des mots dont les orthographes so différentes mais qui ont la même prononciation. Exemple e français d'homophones : *les, lait, laid...* Trouve pour chaqu mot de la liste de droite son homophone dans la liste de gauc et écris-le dans l'espace central. Il te faut donc pronon chaque mot à haute voix.

air		aunt
aren't		are
ate		by
buy		cereal
C		eight
colonel		eye
cue		flower
ewe		four
flour		guest
for		heir
genes		here
guessed		jeans
hear		kernel
I		new
knight		night
knows		nose
knew		one
pair		pear
peace		piece
principle		principal
Q		queue
R		right
rap		see
serial		sight
site		tea
T		too
two		witch
U		wore
war		wrap
which		Y
why		you
won		right
write		you

JE FAIS LE POINT...

SPÉCIAL BREVET

JE COMPRENDS CE QUE J'ENTENDS

1 J'écoute et je copie les phrases. PISTE 30 — /5

1. ....
2. ....
3. ....
4. ....
5. ....

2 Je trouve l'intrus dans ces 5 séries de 5 mots. PISTE 31 — /5

1. a lorry	a taxi	a bus	a car	a helicopter
2. a dentist	a doctor	a vet	a butcher	a pharmacist
3. a zoo	a school	a university	a college	a classroom
4. an elephant	a flying fish	an antelope	a zebra	a buffalo
5. a boy	a girl	a chimpanzee	a baby	a teenager

JE COMPRENDS CE QUE JE LIS

3 Je traduis ces phrases en commençant par « on » suivi d'une forme active. /5

1. I was offered a job yesterday. ....
2. Cheap cars are made in India ....
3. Most toys are sold in supermarkets. ....
4. Tea is produced in India. ....
5. Men will be sent to Mars in a few years. ....

4 Je sais dire si ces phrases sont exactes ou fausses. /10

	True	False
1. France is the most populated country in Europe.		
2. The English and the French used to be enemies.		
3. Russia is the biggest country in the world.		
4. You were born in the nineteenth century.		
5. The river Loire is the longest river in France.		
6. The Pacific Ocean is the largest ocean in the world.		
7. There used to be kangaroos in Scotland.		
8. America was discovered in the fifteenth century.		
9. This is the last exercise of your book.		
10. February is the shortest month of the year.		

5 Je choisis le relatif qui convient.

1. I don't know a. what / b. where / c. why to do now.
2. Australia is a country a. which / b. where / c. when I'd like to go and live.
3. I can't understand a. when / b. Ø / c. why he's always late.
4. The policeman a. where / b. Ø / c. who I met told me he knew you.
5. I can't remember the name of that actor a. who / b. what / c. which advertises for coffee on TV.

| 5

JE COMPRENDS ET J'ÉCRIS

6 Je sais passer de la voix active à la voix passive.

1. They refused his proposal. ....
2. They have arrested her. ....
3. They sell bikes in that shop. ....
4. They will forgive you. ....
5. They have killed my favourite zebra. ....

| 5

7 Je retrouve la forme directe qui a inspiré ces phrases.

| 10

1. He told me to sit down. ....!
2. He asked me what my name was. ....?
3. He asked me how old I was. ....?
4. He wanted to know if I was married. ....?
5. I answered I was. ....
6. He asked me how many children I had. ....?
7. I answered I didn't have any. ....
8. He told me he needed a good lorry driver. ....
9. I said I could drive any vehicle. ....
10. He said I had the job. ....

8 Je sais traduire ces phrases.

1. La plupart de ces chemises sont fabriquées en Inde. ....
2. Cette maison a été construite en 2001. ....
3. Dans le temps j'écrivais des poèmes. ....
4. Tu n'as pas travaillé hier, n'est-ce pas ? ....
5. Il m'a dit qu'il était le meilleur chanteur au monde.
....

| 5

TOTALISE TES POINTS ET MULIPLIE LE TOTAL PAR 2 POUR OBTENIR TON TAUX DE RÉUSSITE

| 50

x 2 =

% de réussite

Entre 100% et 80%, tu as tout compris. BRAVO !
Entre 80% et 60%, c'est bien.
Si tu as moins de 60%, refais les tests dans quelques jours.

- **LE GÉRONDIF**
- **LES ADVERBES**
- **LA FORME EXCLAMATIVE**

unit 11

I love chatting on the net

JE COMPRENDS CE QUE J'ENTENDS

PISTE 32

1 True or false?

	True	False
1. Meet your Idol *is a radio programme.*		
2. Britney Lance is a pop singer.		
3. Bruce is the name of the presenter.		
4. Scott Shane is a lorry driver and a fan of Britney Lance.		
5. He listens to Britney's music when he drives his lorry.		
6. Britney Lance is going to act in a science-fiction film.		
7. Britney doesn't want to be an actress.		
8. Britney is angry when Scott asks his second question.		
9. Scott asks Britney to marry him.		
10. Britney agrees to marry him.		

MON SCORE ..... /10

REMEMBER!

LE GÉRONDIF

En ajoutant ***-ing* à un verbe d'action**, avec ou sans complément, on **renvoie à une activité** :
reading : la lecture *swimming :* la natation *collecting stamps :* faire collection de timbres
Cette forme verbale peut, comme un nom, avoir la fonction d'un sujet ou d'un complément.
***Playing** the organ is my favourite hobby.* Jouer de l'orgue est mon passe-temps favori.
*I practise **fencing** and **riding**.* Je pratique l'escrime et l'équitation.
Certains verbes sont suivis du gérondif ou de l'infinitif du verbe. Le sens est en général différent. La forme en *-ing* correspond à ce qui est fait habituellement, l'infinitif à ce qui va se faire.
He stopped drinking. Il s'est arrêté de boire. *He stopped to drink.* Il s'est arrêté pour boire.
*I like **writing** poems.* J'aime écrire des poèmes. *I'd like **to write** poems.* J'aimerais écrire des poèmes.

MON SCORE ..... /5

PISTE 33

2 Complete these sentences.

Écoute et écris les deux gérondifs qui manquent dans chacune de ces phrases.

1. *My hobbies are* .... *dinosaurs and* .... *horror films.*
2. *I have two jobs:* .... *old fridges and* .... *them.*
3. *I enjoy* .... *in London and* .... *eccentric clothes.*
4. .... *the gorillas and* .... *tourism are Rwanda's chief projects.*
5. .... *and* .... *in a big city is both stressful and exciting.*

REMEMBER!

LES ADVERBES

On forme la plupart des adverbes en **ajoutant *-ly* à un adjectif** : *probably / certainly / definitely / strangely / usually*

les adverbes de manière et d'intensité se placent en général **après** le verbe. *He works **fast** and **efficiently**.* Il travaille vite et efficacement. *She didn't eat **very much**.* Elle n'a pas beaucoup mangé.

Les adverbes de fréquence et de probabilité se placent en général **avant** le verbe sauf avec *be*.

*He **always/often/sometimes** comes on Sundays.* Il vient toujours/souvent/parfois le dimanche.

*He will **certainly** agree.* Il sera certainement d'accord. *He is **never** late.* Il n'est jamais en retard.

3 a or b?

MON SCORE | 5

Place ces adverbes à l'endroit qui convient.

1. *Never → They a. .... came back b. .... from Australia.*
2. *Much → He doesn't a. .... work b.........................., does he?*
3. *Probably → They will a. .... get married b. .... before Christmas.*
4. *Yesterday → The murderer was a. .... arrested in London b. ....*
5. *sometimes → They a. .... were b. .... late for school.*

4 a or b?

MON SCORE | 10

Choisis le mot exact pour compléter ces 10 citations.

1. *I love children... a. boiled. / b. when they're asleep.* W.C. Fields
2. *To be or not to be, that is the a. question / b. problem.* W. Shakespeare
3. *All animals are equal but some animals are a. less / b. more equal than others.* G. Orwell
4. *And so my fellow Americans, ask not what your a. president / b. country can do for you but what you can do for your a. president / b. country.* J.F. Kennedy
5. *The secret of education is respecting a. the pupil / b. the teacher.* R.W. Emerson
6. *People have one thing in common: they are all a. the same / b. different.* R. Zend
7. *That's one small step for a. me / b. man, one giant step for mankind.* N. Armstrong
8. *I don't mind living in a man's world as long as I can be a. a man / b. a woman in it.* Marilyn Monroe
9. *The first half of our lives is ruined by our parents, and the second half by our a. illnesses / b. children.* C. Darrow
10. *We have really everything in common with America except, of course a. language. / b. history.* O. Wilde

5 What am I?

MON SCORE | 5

Complète ces phrases par le mot qui convient.

Customer / passenger / patient / viewer / witness

1. *I'm buying clothes in a shop. I'm a ....*
2. *I'm quite ill and I'm in a hospital. I'm a ....*
3. *I've just seen an accident happen. I'm a ....*
4. *I'm flying to Los Angeles. I'm a ....*
5. *I watch television. I'm a ....*

6 What or How?

Complète ces phrases par *What* ou *How*.

1. .... ridiculous!

2. .... a strange story they told me!

3. .... frightening you look tonight, Count Dracula!

4. .... a weird president you chose!

5. .... a mess! You have 10 minutes to tidy your room!

MON SCORE | 5

REMEMBER!

LA FORME EXCLAMATIVE

Elle se forme avec ***What*** ou ***How***.

What est suivi de *a(an)/ø* + nom/adjectif+nom + !
Le groupe verbal est en général sous-entendu.
What a mistake (that was)! Quelle erreur (ce fut) !
What a silly game! Quel jeu idiot !
What courage (you had)! Quel courage (tu as eu) !
What beautiful children! Quels beaux enfants !

How est suivi d'un adjectif ou d'un adverbe. Le groupe verbal est aussi souvent sous-entendu.
How beautiful she is! Comme elle est belle !
How awful! Comme c'est épouvantable !
How fast he runs! Comme il court vite !

Ne confonds pas :
How old he is! Comme il est vieux !
How old is he? Quel âge a-t-il ?

7 Translate these sentences.

1. La lecture est mon passe-temps favori. ....
2. Je déteste faire la cuisine. ....
3. J'aime ne rien faire. ....
4. J'ai commencé à skier quand j'avais trois ans. ....
5. Elle passe son temps à surfer sur Internet. ....

MON SCORE | 5

8 Make sentences.

1. ridiculous / friends / spend / it / to / how / is / time / your / chatting / with/ !

....

2. Friday / he / rarely / on / works / afternoons/ .

....

3. horrible / what / kids / !

....

4. stupid / seemed / she / to / how / me /!

....

5. mystery / 's / no / good / it / a / trying / to / to / find solution / this /.

....

MON SCORE | 5

CALCULE TON TAUX DE RÉUSSITE SUR CE CHAPITRE

Entre 100% et 80%, tu as tout compris. BRAVO !
Entre 80% et 60%, c'est bien.
Si tu as moins de 60%, refais les tests dans quelques jours.

	___ / 10	1
+	___ / 5	2
+	___ / 5	3
+	___ / 10	4
+	___ / 5	5
+	___ / 5	6
+	___ / 5	7
+	___ / 5	8
=	___ / 50	

x 2 =

___ % de réussite

GAMES!

DES JEUX !

Trouve pour chaque mot des trois colonnes du haut son synonyme dans les trois colonnes du bas.

Accept
Allow
Answer
Attractive
Beat
Begin
Believe
Big
Burst
Change
Cry
Dangerous
Destroy
Difficult
Discover
Enough
Expensive

Extinct
False
Fast
Forbid
Freedom
Funny
Great
Happen
Happy
Hate
Leave
Like Best
Like
Little
Mad
Many
Observe

Present
Pretty
Propose
Rich
Scared
Seat
Seem
Show
Shut
Simple
Supporter
Talk
Tell
True
Unusual
Warm

Afraid
Amusing
Approve
Beautiful
Chair
Charming
Chat
Close
Costly
Crazy
Dead
Depart
Detest
Display
Easy
Excellent
Explode
Find

Gift
Glad
Hard
Hot
Large
Liberty
Look
Love
Modify
Numerous
Partisan
Perceive
Permit
Prefer
Prohibit
Quick
Right
Risky

Ruin
Say
Solution
Start
Strange
Strike
Sufficient
Suggest
Take Place
Think
Wealthy
Weep
Wrong
Young

▸ DONNER UN ORDRE OU FAIRE UNE SUGGESTION
▸ PRÉPOSITIONS ET PARTICULES
▸ RAPPEL DES FORMES VERBALES

What about having a break?

unit 12

JE COMPRENDS CE QUE J'ENTENDS

PISTE 34

1 True or false?

	True	False
1. This conversation takes place in a computer shop.		
2. The customer wants to buy a computer.		
3. He knows a lot about computers.		
4. The shop-assistant wants to sell him a car.		
5. The customer needs a computer he can travel with.		
6. He wants a small screen.		
7. The shop-assistant tells him he can have a printer for $100.		
8. The customer is also buying software.		
9. He's going to spend about $1,500.		
10. He's going to have coffee with the shop-assistant.		

MON SCORE | 10

REMEMBER!

DONNER UN ORDRE OU FAIRE UNE SUGGESTION

L'impératif se forme à la 2e personne à l'aide de la base verbale. *Look!* Regarde ! *Repeat!* Répète !
À la forme négative, la base verbale est précédée de *Don't*. *Don't talk!* Ne bavardez pas !
La 1re personne du pluriel se forme avec *Let's* (=*Let us*) à la forme affirmative ou ***Let's not*** à la forme négative suivi de la base verbale. *Let's go home!* Rentrons à la maison !
Let's not talk of her again! Ne reparlons pas d'elle !
Les verbes suivis d'une préposition ne gardent que la base verbale. *Listen!* Écoute ! mais *Listen to me!*
Au contraire, les verbes suivis d'un adverbe (particule) le conservent. *Come in!* Entre !
On peut suggérer, de façon plus ou moins autoritaire, de faire quelque chose.
What about going to bed? Si tu allais te coucher ?
How about reading a good book for a change? Pourquoi ne pas lire un bon livre pour changer ?
Shall we go? On s'en va ?

PISTE 35

2 What do they mean?

MON SCORE | 5

Écoute et dis ce que tu comprends.

1. a. Someone will open the door for me. / b. I'll have to open the door.
2. a. We spend a lot of time at home. / b. We go out a lot.
3. a. I can do what I like with my money. / b. I can't buy what I like.
4. a. My teacher wants me to keep quiet. / b. My teacher likes what I'm saying.
5. a. My friend would like to stop working. / b. My friend wants to go on working.

JE COMPRENDS CE QUE JE LIS

REMEMBER!

PRÉPOSITIONS ET PARTICULES

Une préposition introduit un complément. *Listen to me!* Écoute-moi !
Sans complément, la préposition disparaît dans une phrase affirmative ou négative mais subsiste dans une phrase interrogative. *Listen!* Écoute ! *What are you listening to?* Qu'est-ce que tu écoutes ?
Une particule modifie le sens d'un verbe. *Switch on/off the television.* Allume/Éteins la télévision.
Un pronom complément se place entre le verbe et la particule.
Put your shoes on! / Put them on! Mets tes chaussures ! / Mets-les !
Certains verbes peuvent être suivis d'une particule et d'une préposition.
Get out of your room! Sors de ta chambre !
He'll come back from England tomorrow. Il reviendra demain d'Angleterre.

MON SCORE | 10

3 Translate these sentences.

1. *Who does this phone belong to?* ....
2. *What time did your plane take off?* ....
3. *He doesn't look at all like his father.* ....
4. *I want my money back!* ....
5. *He swam across the lake in ten minutes.* ....
6. *What does your ice-cream taste like?* ....
7. *He climbed up the tree and fell down.* ....
8. *Do you think of me when I'm away?* ....
9. *Bringing up children isn't always easy.* ....
10. *You'll get used to your maths teacher's sense of humour* ....

4 Who says that?

MON SCORE | 10

Attribue à chaque phrase la profession correspondante.
a banker / a dentist / a mechanic / a movie-director / a pilot /
a reporter / a shop assistant / a surgeon / a taxi driver / a television announcer

1. *Open your mouth and stop shouting! I won't hurt you!* ....
2. *Victoria Station? It'll take at least an hour to get there.*
The traffic is very busy today. ....
3. *Mr President! What do you intend to do for the jobless?* ....
4. *Tell me, Miss! Do you ever check the oil of your car?* ....
5. *This is Captain O'Henry speaking. We'll land in about ten minutes at Kennedy airport. Will you please fasten your safety belts.* ....
6. *Can I help you? This computer is a real bargain. It's only £499.* ....
7. *I'm afraid we'll have to operate on you. You'll feel much better afterwards.* ....
8. *Cut!... Really, Angelina, try to remember you're supposed to be an actress!* ....
9. *Here is the news. The Prime Minister is to meet the French President in Brussels this afternoon.* ....
10. *I'm sorry but we can't lend you £1,000,000. We think your project is unrealistic.* ....

JE SAIS M'EXPRIMER

REMEMBER!

RAPPEL DES FORMES VERBALES

L'expression du présent *I never get up before 11 on Sunday.* Je ne me lève jamais avant 11h le dimanche. *Oh, no! It's raining again!* Oh, non ! Il pleut encore ! *Congratulations! You've won the match!* Félicitations ! Tu as gagné le match ! *I've been waiting for one hour.* J'attends depuis une heure.
L'expression du passé *I broke my arm last Saturday.* Je me suis cassé le bras samedi dernier.
It was freezing when I arrived. Il gelait quand je suis arrivé.
I had never seen a giraffe before. Je n'avais jamais vu de girafe auparavant.
He had been waiting for an hour when she arrived. Il l'attendait depuis une heure quand elle est arrivée.
He used to play football. Dans le temps il jouait au football.
L'expression du futur *I'll come to your party but I won't dance.* Je viendrai à ta fête mais je ne danserai pas.
I'll start when I'm ready. Je commencerai quand je serai prêt. *I'm going to buy a new computer.* Je vais acheter un nouvel ordinateur. *They're arriving tomorrow afternoon.* Ils arrivent demain après-midi.
L'expression du conditionnel *I'd (= I would) help you if I could.* Je t'aiderais si je pouvais.
Fred would have liked to see you. Fred aurait aimé te voir.

5 *Complete these sentences.*

Complète ces 10 phrase par l'une des 10 possibilités suivantes.
are you going / Does he watch / I'd like / I'll marry / I've been working / I've bought / Someone's crying / There used to be / were the children doing / wrote

1. What .... when the teacher opened the door?
2. .... TV every evening?
3. .... to speak to that boy. He's cute!
4. .... for five hours. I'm tired!
5. Look ! .... a fantastic racket. I'm going to win the match.
6. .... pirates in the Caribbean Islands.
7. .... you when I'm rich!
8. Corneille .... Le Cid in 1636.
9. Listen! .... upstairs!
10. Jane! What .... to do with that revolver?

MON SCORE | 10

6 *Make sentences.*

1. Emma / does / her / look / mother / like / ?

....

2. change / a / for / restaurant / good / a / to / going / about / how / ?

....

3. in / subject / are / interested / you / what / ?

....

4. said / he / he / me / was / with / disappointed / .

....

5. book / the / don't / me / this / last / exercise / tell / of / is / the / !

....

MON SCORE | 5

CALCULE TON TAUX DE RÉUSSITE SUR CE CHAPITRE

Entre 100% et 80%, tu as tout compris. BRAVO !
Entre 80% et 60%, c'est bien.
Si tu as moins de 60%, refais les tests dans quelques jours.

	___ / 10	1
+	___ / 5	2
+	___ / 10	3
+	___ / 10	4
+	___ / 10	5
+	___ / 5	6
=	___ / 50	

x 2 =

___ % de réussite

GAMES! DES JEUX !

What kind of kid are you? Know more about yourself.

1. Your favourite school activity is
a. maths / b. sport / c. drama / d. technology

2. Your favourite sport is
a. tennis. / b. football. / c. table-tennis. / d. jogging.

3. Your favourite pet is
a. a cat. / b. a dog. / c. a snake. / d. a goldfish.

4. Your favourite food is
a. fish / b. hamburgers. / c. caviar. / d. pizza.

5. On Sundays you
a. get up at 6 and read. / b. go jogging. / c. go to the drama club. / d. fix your computer.

6. You read
a. encyclopedias. / b. sports magazines. / c. Shakespeare's plays. / d. mangas.

7. You think you are
a. bright. / b. the best. / c. attractive. / d. practical.

8. Your friends say
a. you know too much. / b. you run fast. / c. you're a show off. / d. you're helpful.

9. Your parents would like you
a. to do sports. / b. to try to read a book. / c. to shut up. / d. to meet friends.

10. You think that one day you could
a. be a Nobel prize winner. / b. be a great champion. / c. be a star. / d. be a new Bill Gates.

You got mostly a's.
OK, you're a bright kid but are you really popular in your class? Practise a team sport and take an interest in the people around you.

You got mostly b's.
Sport is OK but there are lots of things you could also try. What about reading a book or going to the cinema?

You got mostly C's.
No doubt you'll be a great star in Hollywood one day but stop acting all the time. It's exhausting for the people around you.

You got mostly d's.
You seem to be a nice person but you can't spend your life with computers. Go out, meet people and buy some fashionable clothes.

You got a mixture of a's, b's, C's and d's.
Well you seem to be the average sort of teenager. Sorry...

JE FAIS LE POINT…

SPÉCIAL BREVET

JUIN

JE COMPRENDS CE QUE J'ENTENDS

1 J'écoute et je copie les phrases. PISTE 36 — /5

1. ………………………………………………… .
2. ………………………………………………… .
3. ………………………………………………… .
4. ………………………………………………… .
5. ………………………………………………… .

2 Je comprends ce que veut dire mon interlocuteur. PISTE 37 — /5

1. a. He's pleased with me. / b. He thinks I'm not very clever.
2. a. He wants me to help my mother. / b. He wants my mother to help me.
3. a. He wants to know how old she is. / b. He thinks she's very old.
4. a. He says he likes running. / b. He asks me to go jogging with him.
5. a. He likes my girlfriend. / b. He doesn't like my girlfriend.

JE COMPRENDS CE QUE JE LIS

3 Je choisis la particule qui convient quand elle est nécessaire. — /10

1. – Knock! Knock! – Come a. in! / b. on! / c. out!
2. Hurry a. off! / b. on! / c. up! We're late!
3. Why didn't you wait a. for / b. to / c. at me after the match?
4. She said she didn't approve a. in / b. for / c. of my reaction.
5. I agree a. of / b. with / c. about you.
6. I heard a. for / b. of / c. to my favourite actor on the radio this morning.
7. Are you good a. in / b. at / c. on maths?
8. I'm sorry I can't put you a. up / b. in / c. away. My house is too small.
9. Everything depends a. of / b. to / c. on your school results.
10. Switch a. on / b. off / c. down the TV and go to bed.

4 Je trouve à quel gérondif correspondent ces définitions d'activités courantes. — /5

1. Running at a slow and regular pace, often alternatively with walking. ……………… .
2. Visiting stores and shops to look at things and sometimes buying them. ……………… .
3. The art of preparing food for the table usually done in a kitchen. ……………… .
4. Moving along in water by using arms and legs. ……………… .
5. Reproducing cars, ships, planes or buildings as a hobby. ……………… .

5 Je comprends et je traduis.

| 5

1. Finding your way on the London Tube isn't very easy.

....

2. How wonderful it was seeing you! ....

3. He'd never thought of leaving his job in Wall Street.

....

4. Are you sure you'll get used to looking after six rottweilers?

....

5. If only I hadn't answered the phone that day! ....

JE COMPRENDS ET J'ÉCRIS

6 Je sais traduire ces phrases.

| 10

1. Comme c'est intéressant ! ....

2. Il adore jouer du violon. ....

3. Quelle erreur ! ....

4. D'habitude, elle se lève à 8 heures. ....

5. Que dirais-tu d'aller au zoo ? ....

6. Traduis ce texte en italien. ....

7. Je ne l'avais jamais vue. ....

8. Quel dommage que tu ne puisses venir ! ....

9. Elle n'est pas habituée à travailler avec lui. ....

10. Est-ce qu'il a plu souvent en juillet ? ....

7 Je sais compléter ces phrases par 10 auxiliaires différents à la forme qui convient.

| 10

1. Your parents .... agree, won't they?

2. He spoke English, ... he?

3. .... he waiting for you at the airport when you arrived?

4. I' .... go home right now if I could.

5. It's a pity you .... drive. I thought of giving you my old car.

6. – What job .... he do? – He's a guitar player.

7. Are you sure he' .... really understood what he has to do now?

8. That man .... always complaining! It's exhausting!

9. Why .... dogs allowed in restaurants?

10. She'....................... spent all her pocket money when she came back home.

TOTALISE TES POINTS ET MULIPLIE LE TOTAL PAR 2 POUR OBTENIR TON TAUX DE RÉUSSITE

| 50

x 2 =

% de réussite

Entre 100% et 80%, tu as tout compris. BRAVO !
Entre 80% et 60%, c'est bien.
Si tu as moins de 60%, refais les tests dans quelques jours.